GW00418810

LONDON
Atlas & Guide

Contents

Published by Collins
An imprint of HarperCollinsPublishers
77-85 Fulham Palace Road, Hammersmith, London W6 8JB

Collins® is a registered trademark of HarperCollinsPublishers Limited
Copyright © HarperCollinsPublishers Ltd 2003
www.collins.co.uk

Mapping generated from Collins Bartholomew digital databases

Text on pages 3-57 researched and written by Karen Lloyd

London Underground Map by permission of Transport Trading Limited Registered User No. 04/3901

The grid on this mapping is the National Grid taken from the Ordnance Survey map with the permission of the Controller of Her Majesty's Stationery Office.

Printed in Hong Kong   ISBN 0 00 716951 5   QN11593 EDM   Imp 001   e-mail: roadcheck@harpercollins.co.uk

London guide

Symbols used in the text

  Disabled facilities available. This does not necessarily mean that
facilities are not available elsewhere. Always check before travelling.

  London is full of fascinating things for children to see and do.
This guide suggests just some of them with this symbol.

  Buying a London Pass can be a cost effective way of seeing many
of the capital's sights. For more details see page 7.

  This symbol gives an indication of some of London's best known
attractions. They are places not to miss on your trip to London.

Essential Information

Emergencies

The freephone numbers to use if someone is in immediate danger, or a crime is happening, are **999** or **112**. You will speak to an operator who will ask you if you need the police, ambulance or fire brigade. Keep calm, answer their questions carefully and help will soon be with you.

Accidents & ill health

◆ Hospitals

Holiday visitors, EU citizens and people from countries with reciprocal arrangements can receive free medical treatment at National Health Service (NHS) hospitals. Non-EU citizens can have free emergency treatment only in the Accident and Emergency (A&E) departments of NHS hospitals; if you need to be admitted to a ward, you will be charged. You will also be charged for any other treatment unless you have medical insurance. The following central London hospitals have A&E departments:

Chelsea & Westminster, Fulham Road, SW10	☎ 020 7746 8000
Guy's, St. Thomas Street, SE1	☎ 020 7955 5000
St. Mary's, Praed Street, W2	☎ 020 7886 6666
St. Thomas', Lambeth Palace Road, SE1	☎ 020 7928 9292
University College, Grafton Way, WC1	☎ 020 7387 9300

◆ Dentists

Emergency dental treatment can be obtained from:
Charing Cross Emergency Dental Clinic (outside the area of this guide)
Charing Cross Hospital, Fulham Palace Road, SW6   ☎ 020 8846 1005

◆ Doctors & chemists

If you have a minor illness or ailment, either telephone the 24 hour NHS Direct helpline (☎ 0845 4647), or go to any chemists' shop (pharmacy/drugstore) where the pharmacist will be able to help you. The local police station will have a list of doctors in the area and if you need medication after normal closing time (5pm to 6pm), they will also have a list of late night chemists. In central London this will include:

Bliss chemists, 5-6 Marble Arch, W1	☎ 020 7723 6116
Boots chemists, Piccadilly Circus, W1	☎ 020 7734 6126
Boots chemists, 74 Queensway, W2	☎ 020 7229 9266
Tesco Metro, 311 Oxford Street, WC1	☎ 020 7530 8400

Car breakdown

◆ Breakdown organisations

If you are not already a member you can join some breakdown organisations at the roadside. There may be a surcharge for these services, so check when telephoning. The following telephone numbers are for use in the event of a breakdown:

Automobile Association (AA)	☎ 0800 887766
Green Flag	☎ 0800 400600
More Than	☎ 0800 300988
Royal Automobile Association (RAC)	☎ 0800 828282

◆ Garages

Recovery services are also available from some local garages. Always ask for prices.

24 Hour Breakdown, Eaton Mews, Eaton Square, SW1	☎ 020 7235 1954
A & B Recovery, 8 The Tarns, Varndell Street, NW1	☎ 020 7387 9439
Rapid Recovery, Wyndham Road, SE5	☎ 020 7277 1142

Lost property

Apply to the nearest police station. Lost property found in the street is usually taken there. For property lost in other locations:

Black Cab, underground or bus.
The Lost Property Office, 200 Baker Street, NW1. Allow 24 hours before enquiring. The office is open 9am to 2pm Mon to Fri. A charge is made on collection. ☎ 020 7918 2000

Docklands Light Railway.
DLR, Security Hut, Poplar Station. £2 fee. ☎ 020 7363 9550

Gatwick Airport.
Excess Baggage Company, South Terminal. Open 8am to 7pm Mon to Sat, 8am to 4pm Sun. Fee payable. ☎ 0870 0002 468

Heathrow Airport.
Information desk in relevant terminal. After 24 hours, airport Lost Property Office. ☎ 0870 0000 123, ☎ 020 8745 7727

River services.
The boat operator, the pier office. ☎ 020 7941 2400

South West Trains.
South West Trains, Friars Bridge Court, 41-45 Blackfriars Road, SE1 7.30am to 8pm Mon to Fri. ☎ 020 7401 7861

Stansted Airport.
AAS Ltd. Open 9.30am to 4.30pm daily. Items held for three months.
Rising charge depending on how long it takes you to collect - £15 after
3 months.   ☎ 01279 663 293
Victoria Coach Station.
Victoria Coach Station, Help Point. 8am to 8pm every day. £2 fee if
property found.   ☎ 020 7824 0000

If all else fails, contact The Lost Property Office at 200 Baker Street,
NW1. Most things left on public transport arrive there sooner or later!

◆ Lost or stolen credit cards

Immediately report lost or stolen credit cards to the issuing company,
using their emergency phone numbers:

American Express ☎ 01273 696 933	**Mastercard**	☎ 0800 96 4767	
Barclaycard ☎ 01604 230 230	**NatWest**	☎ 0870 600 0459	
HSBC ☎ 0845 600 7010	**Visa**	☎ 0800 89 1725	
Lloyds TSB ☎ 0800 096 9779			

Money

◆ Currency

The pound sterling (£) is divided into 100 pence (p). Coin values are 1p,
2p, 5p, 10p, 20p, 50p, £1 and £2. Notes are £5, £10, £20 and £50.

◆ Banks

Most banks are open on weekdays from 9.30am to 5pm, and have at
least one ATM (cash dispensing machine). Many main branches are also
open for a shorter period on Saturdays. One branch of each of the four
major banks is listed below.

Barclays, 78 Victoria Street, Victoria, SW1   ☎ 0800 400 100
HSBC, 89 Buckingham Palace Road, SW1   ☎ 020 7699 1401
Lloyds TSB, 179 Earls Court Road, SW5   ☎ 0845 300 0033
NatWest, 185 Sloane Street, Knightsbridge, SW1   ☎ 0845 605 1605

◆ Foreign exchange

The best rates of exchange are usually found in banks. However, Bureau
de Change are often open outside banking hours.
The Money Corporation, 18 Piccadilly, W1   ☎ 020 7439 2100
Thomas Exchange Global, 141 Victoria Street, SW1 ☎ 020 7828 1880
TTT Foreign Exchange Corporation,
The Plaza, 120 Oxford Street, W1   ☎ 020 7255 2555

◆ The Euro

Although the UK has not adopted the Euro, many large stores and services will accept it in their larger branches. Look for a sign on the door or ask a member of staff. At London airports, you can use Euros with NCP car parks and you can pay for train tickets in Euros on the Gatwick Express, Virgin Trains and the Stansted Express.

◆ Tax refunds on goods

If you are from a non-EU country, you can reclaim some of the tax you have paid on some of your shopping. Go to **Premier Tax Free**, Maddox Street, W1, for refunds on purchases of less than £1000.
www.premiertaxfree.com

Passports & embassies

◆ Passports

As soon as you can, get a photocopy of the essential parts of your passport, particularly the number. This may speed things up if it needs to be replaced. If you do lose it or it is stolen, inform the local police immediately and contact your embassy or consulate.

◆ Embassies

The London Tourist Board website www.visitlondon.com has a list of all the major embassies in London, some of which are listed below. A London Black Cab taxi driver will always be able to take you to your embassy, even if you do not know the address.

Australia, Australia House, Strand WC2	☎ 020 7379 4334
France, 21 Cromwell Road, SW7	☎ 020 7838 2000
Germany, 23 Belgrave Square, SW1	☎ 020 7824 1300
Japan, 101-104 Piccadilly, W1	☎ 020 7465 6565
South Africa, 15 Whitehall, SW1	☎ 020 7925 8900
United Arab Emirates, 48 Prince's Gate, SW7	☎ 020 7589 3434
USA, 5 Upper Grosvenor Street, W1	☎ 020 7499 9000

Public toilets

Look out for street signs saying 'toilets' or 'public toilets'. Bear in mind that many are locked after dark, except for the 24 hour unisex ones that look like shiny metal cabins; you need exactly the right coins to use these. All other public toilets are separated into male and female and there is sometimes a charge to use them. You will also find them in most public transport stations, except for the underground.

Visitors with disabilities

Some buses, trains and stations have facilities for disabled access, but not all, so it is advisable to check in advance before travelling on public transport. Contact the London Transport Unit ☎ 020 7222 1234. Their free booklet *'Access to the Underground'* is available from London Transport travel information centres. General information and advice is also available from the following organisations:

Artsline (arts and entertainment access), 54 Charlton Street, NW1
www.artsline.org.uk ☎ 020 7388 2227
DIAL (information and advice line) ☎ 01302 310123
Disability Now, 6 Market Road, N7
www.disabilitynow.org.uk ☎ 020 7619 7323

For information on access to theatres www.theatre-access.co.uk
For information on access to restaurants www.viewlondon.co.uk
For information on access to pubs www.pubs.com/disablist.htm

Wheelchair and vehicle hire is available from:
Wheelchair Travel, 1 Johnston Green, Guildford, Surrey ☎ 01483 233640
www.wheelchair-travel.co.uk

Tourist information centres

These can provide you with information on accommodation, trips and tours, current events and so on. If they do not have the answer, they can usually find someone who does. Personal callers are welcome at:
Britain Visitor Centre, 1 Regent Street, Piccadilly Circus, SW1
Heathrow Airport Tourist Information Centre, Underground Station
London Visitor Centre, Arrivals Hall, Waterloo International Terminal
Victoria Tourist Information Centre, Station Forecourt, SW1
Alternatively, phone the London Tourist Board's information line
☎ 09068 663344, calls charged 60p/minute.

The London Pass

For good value on public transport and to beat queues at over 50 attractions, buy a 'London Pass'. You will also get discounts at some theatres and restaurants. You can buy a pass with or without transport, for 1,2,3 or 6 consecutive days. For example:
Without transport for **6** consecutive days   Adult £69.00   Child £37.00
With transport for **6** consecutive days   Adult £107.00   Child £56.00

Attractions shown with a ▭ in this guide are covered by the pass, either for free entrance or discounts on other services. Buy with a credit or debit card ☎ 0870 242 9988, or from any Exchange International, or on-line at www.londonpass.com

When to visit

The following list includes not only the most important annual events but also some of the more obscure and interesting London customs. For exact days, times and places contact the London Tourist Board's information line ☎ 09068 663344, calls charged at 60p/minute.

Annual events

New Year's Day Parade, 1st January.
A huge parade through the West End. All sorts of entertainment including American style marching bands, vintage cars and floats. Free.
Whitehall, through Trafalgar Square, Pall Mall, Piccadilly Circus
www.londonparade.co.uk   ☎ 020 8566 8586

London International Boat Show, early January.
Built over the water, this exhibition venue has floating as well as static displays. Cost on application.
ExCeL, Royal Victoria Dock, E16   ☎ 0115 912 9111
www.excel-london.co.uk

Chinese New Year, February.
Traditional Chinese celebrations. Free.
Around Leicester Square, WC2

The London Marathon, April.
26 mile (42km) race through the streets of London. Spectators free.
Greenwich/Blackheath to The Mall

London Harness Horse Parade, Easter Monday.
Parade of horse drawn vehicles. Free.
Battersea Park, SW11

Chelsea Flower Show, May, over four days.
The garden event of the year. Essential to book in advance. Full sized display gardens, plant companies from all over the world, wonderful scents in the floral pavilion. Plants can be purchased on the last day. Cost on application. No under 5s.
Royal Hospital, Chelsea, SW3   ☎ 0870 906 3781
www.firstcalltickets.com

Beating the Retreat, May or June, two or three evenings, 7pm to 8pm.
Cavalry, Guards and the Corps of Drums play spine tingling military music and drill as the sun sets. Book well in advance. £7 to £10.
Horse Guards Parade, SW1   ☎ 020 7414 2271

Doggett's Coat and Badge Race, July.
The oldest annual sporting event in Britain dating from 1721. Five young men from the Watermen's Company row along the Thames in a race to win Doggett's Coat and Badge. Free.
London Bridge to Cadogan Pier, Chelsea Embankment

☎ 020 7361 2826

Royal Academy Summer Exhibition, June to August.
Works by painters, printmakers and sculptors at this contemporary art exhibition, the largest of its kind in the world. Some pieces are for sale. Cost on application.
Royal Academy, Burlington House,
Piccadilly, W1   ☎ 020 7413 1717

The Queen's Birthday Parade (Trooping the Colour), June.
Although Her Majesty's real birthday is on 21st April, she has an official birthday in June when the weather is, hopefully, better. This is a spectacular show of pageantry, when troops from the Household Division (foot and mounted) are inspected by the Queen who is also in uniform. After the bands have played some stirring music the regimental colour is passed down the ranks; originally, the flags were paraded past the troops so they would recognise them in battle. Finally, the Queen rides back to Buckingham Palace at the head of her Guards. Free.
Horse Guards Parade, SW1

The Proms, July to September.
The Henry Wood Promenade Concerts, a tradition since 1895. Quality classical music for all at low prices. Over 70 performances and always a good atmosphere. Book early. Cost on application.
Royal Albert Hall, Kensington Gore, SW7   ☎ 020 7589 8212

Notting Hill Carnival, August Bank Holiday.
A taste of the Caribbean in one of the world's largest street parties. Free.
Around W11 area

Fireworks Night, around 5th November.
A unique British celebration to commemorate the Gunpowder Plot, when the Houses of Parliament were nearly blown up around 400 years ago. Effigies of the plotters are burnt on a bonfire and fireworks are let off. Cost varies, some free.
Events all over London

London to Brighton Veteran Car Run, first Sunday in November.
A race for cars of pre-1905 vintage. The event celebrates the abolition of the law that required a man with a red flag to walk in front of all cars! Superb old vehicles from all over the world. Free.
Hyde Park (7.30am) to Brighton

State opening of Parliament, October or November.
Although you cannot enter the Houses of Parliament, it is a wonderful opportunity to see the Queen and Duke of Edinburgh travel from Buckingham Palace in the magnificent gold State Coach. Free.
Houses of Parliament, SW1

Lord Mayor's Show, second Saturday in November.
The origins of this parade date from 1215, when the newly elected Mayor of London travelled to the Royal Courts of Justice to pledge allegiance to the Crown. The procession still takes place but now includes bands, floats and other entertainment. Money is collected en route for a charity selected by the Lord Mayor. The grand finale is a firework display over the Thames. Free.
Mansion House to the Royal Courts of Justice, Strand, WC2
www.lordmayorsshow.org ☎ 020 7606 3030

Christmas lights, from the end of November.
Festive illuminations along with beautiful seasonal displays in the windows of all the large department stores; don't miss Hamley's Toy Shop. Free.
Oxford Street, Regent Street and Bond Street, W1

Christmas carols, late December
Westminster Abbey, SW1 ☎ 020 7654 4900
www.westminster-abbey.org

Daily events

◆ Changing of the Guard

Buckingham Palace 📷 11.30am to 12.15pm either every day or alternate days. Cancelled in very wet weather.
The correct name for this ceremony is 'Guard Mounting'. A band accompanies the New Guard as they exchange duties with the Old Guard. The Queen's Guard is usually, but not always, the Foot Guards in the famous red and black uniforms with bearskin hats. Adult £12.00, child £6.00, with concessions, under 5's free. Credit card booking.
SW1 ☎ 020 7321 2233

Horse Guards Parade, 11am Mon to Sat, 10am Sun. Dismount ceremony daily at 4pm. Phone London Tourist Board first to check times.
The Queen's Life Guard ride on splendid horses from Hyde Park Barracks at 10.28am Mon to Sat and 9.28am Sun. They pass Hyde Park Corner, Constitution Hill and The Mall, arriving at Horse Guards Arch where the ceremony takes place.
Whitehall, SW1

Tower of London, 11.30am. Phone London Tourist Board first to check times.
A small ceremony with fifteen men, one officer and five non-commissioned officers.
Tower Hill, EC3

St. James's Palace, 10.45am to 11am. Phone London Tourist Board first to check times.
Part of the Old Guard marches from St. James's Palace to Buckingham Palace.
SW1

◆ The Ceremony of the Keys

Tower of London, nightly at 9.53pm.
The ancient ceremony of locking the Tower for the night. The Chief Warder walks from the Byward Tower carrying a candle lantern and the Queen's Keys. Various gates are locked en route, with all guards and sentries saluting the Keys. When they return to the Bloody Tower, the sentry there calls out a challenge, once satisfied that these are the Queen's Keys, the Chief Warder is allowed to proceed up the steps and calls *God preserve Queen Elizabeth*, the officer in charge replies *Amen*. The clock chimes ten and the Last Post is played.
Tower Hill, EC3

◆ Speakers' Corner

Marble Arch, any time of day.
A remaining vestige of the British tradition of free speech is this institution of impromptu discourses by various speakers, usually on politics or religion. Free.
Marble Arch, corner of Hyde Park, W2

Getting around

From airports to the city

London City Airport ☎ 020 7646 0088
Rail from Silvertown to Fenchurch Street station ☎ 08457 48 49 50.
Shuttlebus to Liverpool Street station.

London Gatwick Airport ☎ 0870 000 2468
Rail departure from south terminal to Victoria (non stop)
☎ 01293 53 53 53 www.gatwickexpress.co.uk. Alternatively there is a
Thameslink train to London Bridge, Blackfriars and King's Cross
www.thameslink.co.uk or an airbus connection to Victoria
www.airbus.co.uk

London Heathrow Airport ☎ 0870 0000 123
Underground connections at all terminals. There is also an express rail
service to Paddington ☎ 0845 600 1515 www.heathrowexpress.co.uk
and an airbus service to King's Cross and central London
☎ 020 7222 1234 www.airbus.co.uk

London Stansted Airport ☎ 0870 0000 303
Rail to Liverpool Street ☎ 08457 48 49 50 www.stanstedexpress.co.uk.
Airbus connection to Victoria www.airbus.co.uk

Public transport

◆ Buses

There are two types of buses in London. Basically, if you get on at the
front, you pay the driver, if you board at the back, you take a seat and
pay a conductor. There are also two types of bus stop, the white circle
with white bar on a red background, where a bus will always stop (unless
it is full) and the same symbol with REQUEST written on the
white bar where a bus will only stop if you hold out your arm to show
the driver you want to be picked up. Each stop has a destination list
along with the number of the bus; this information is repeated on the
front of the bus. Ring the bell when you want to get off. Within zone 1,
all journeys cost £1, in zones 2 to 6 the fare is 70p. Night buses run from
11pm to 6am from bus stop signs with a dark blue background and
yellow writing. The London Transport Travel Information Centre
☎ 020 7222 1234 will answer queries about timetables and fares and
give journey planning advice.

◆ Riverside buses ♿

This route links forty tourist attractions, five river piers, three rail stations and five tube stations. All buses are low floor and accessible for the disabled. The buses run every 10 minutes at peak times, linking Tower Gateway, London Bridge station, Bankside, Waterloo station and Covent Garden.

◆ The Underground

The London Underground system, commonly known as the 'Tube', is the simplest way of getting around London and is a particularly efficient way to travel in the area of central London covered by this atlas. There are 12 lines with 273 stations. Each line is colour coded and maps of the network are displayed in the stations and on the trains. The best value ticket is the Travelcard, or buy a ticket at a ticket office or automatic machine at the station. There are six travel zones, and fares are linked to how many zones are travelled through. Tubes start running around 5.30am during the week and continue up to midnight. The Jubilee line has wheelchair accessible trains and stations can be accessed by lift. Most other stations have stairs or escalators, check the website for accessibility.

www.londontransport.co.uk or www.thetube.com ☎ 020 7222 1234

◆ Rail

The Mainline stations in London are Paddington (serving the west), Euston, St. Pancras and King's Cross (north), Liverpool Street (east), Waterloo (south west) and London Bridge, Charing Cross and Victoria (south). Tickets can be bought from a travel agent or rail station and Travelcards can be used within the six London zones. All Eurostar trains, which run from Waterloo, are wheelchair accessible. ☎ 08457 48 49 50

◆ Coach

Victoria Coach Station in Buckingham Palace Road is the main coach station for National Express Coaches. Tickets can be purchased at the coach station (6am to 11.30pm daily), or ☎ 020 7730 3499.

◆ Docklands Light Railway (DLR) ♿

Built in 1987 to serve the Docklands area in East London, this system connects with the Underground system and runs from Bank to Beckton, with an extension south to Lewisham. The trains, in their red, white and blue livery are computer-controlled but do have a guard/ticket-collector on board. Travelcards are accepted. Wheelchair friendly. www.dlr.co.uk

Travelcards & the London Pass

◆ Travelcards

These are daily, weekly or monthly passes (you need a passport sized photo for the last two) which allow unlimited travel on all public transport within particular zones. You can buy them at newsagents displaying a *'pass agent'* sign, or in rail and tube stations or in some Tourist Information Centres.

◆ London 'Rail & Sail' tickets

A ticket gives you one day's unlimited travel on City Cruises River Boats and Docklands Light Railway ☎ 020 7222 1234 or www.dlr.co.uk

◆ The London Pass

Purchase of the London Pass gives free travel on buses, trains, Docklands Light Rail, Tramlink and the Underground. See the 'Essential information' section for details.

Taxis

The London 'Black Cabs' are not necessarily black any more, but if you want to travel in safety, with a driver who knows the streets of London thoroughly, use them. All these cabs have a yellow 'For Hire' sign, if it is lit up, they are free for hire. Hail one by waving, or you will find them at taxi ranks. There are also private hire cabs but do not hire one in the street as you have no guarantee they are operating legally, it is safest to phone for one. Always ask about fares before travelling.

London Black Cabs ♿
Charges are by meter and are displayed in the cab. All have wheelchair ramps and other aids for the disabled. They run 24 hours a day, all year.

www.londonblackcabs.co.uk	☎ 07957 696673
Computer Cab	☎ 020 7432 1432
Dial a Cab	☎ 020 7253 5000
Radio Taxis	☎ 020 7272 0272

Car hire

Driving in London really is not much fun, especially in the rush hour. However, if you want a day out in the country, you could always hire a car. It is advisable to use a firm belonging to the British Vehicle Renting and Leasing Association (BVRLA).

Avis Rent a Car 181-183 Warwick Road, W14   ☎ 020 7244 6577
Europcar 129 Wilton Road, SW1   ☎ 020 7834 8484
Hertz Rent a Car 200a Buckingham Palace Road, SW1   ☎ 020 7730 8323
Sixt Kenning 7-11 South Lambeth Place, SW8   ☎ 020 7582 1769

Different companies have different requirements, but for most you will
need to be over 25; you will also require a driving licence. Check the car
for damage before you leave and make sure this is documented. Finally,
remember, drive on the left hand side of the road!

Driving around London

◆ Congestion charges

A charging zone encompasses the area of inner London. The £5 charge
to enter this area applies only on weekdays between 7am and 6.30pm.
Blue/orange badge holders from the EU are exempt provided they have
registered and paid the one-off £10 charge. ☎ 0845 900 1234 or pay
online at www.cclondon.com. Alternatively, pay at various outlets such
as petrol stations, newsagents etc. displaying the PayPoint logo.

◆ Parking

Parking spaces in London are few and expensive. The maximum stay is
usually around two hours on a meter and most areas are restricted with
double yellow (no parking at any time) or single yellow lines (no
parking during working hours). You cannot park on a 'Red Route' at
any time. Illegal parking can result in fines, wheel clamping or towing
away. If your car has been towed away ☎ 020 7747 7474. If you are
'clamped' on private property, it could cost you £100 to be freed.
Privately run car parks (**NCP** ☎ 0870 606 7050 and **Masterpark**
☎ 0800 243 348 for example) are located all over the city.

Bicycle hire

Cycling in central London is not for the faint-hearted and not
recommended for children. The roads are busy but the parks and
quieter areas can be pleasant. You can just hire a bike or have a guided
tour with a group.
The London Bicycle Tour Company 🚲 1a Gabriel's Wharf, SE1
www.londonbicycle.com   ☎ 020 7928 6838
On Your Bike 52-54 Tooley Street, SE1
www.onyourbike.net   ☎ 020 7378 6669

Places to stay

London offers a broad range of places to stay. The most expensive hotel accommodation is in the West End, with prices decreasing with distance from the centre. Self-catering could also be an option to consider. If you are on a tight budget, there are hostels, or even student Halls of Residence out of term time.

Booking accommodation

If you haven't already booked somewhere to stay, try the London Tourist Board booking service or an accommodation agency. There is usually a booking charge.

◆ Accommodation agencies & booking services

British Hotel Reservation Centre
Huge range. If you are not sure what you want, an advisor will help you. 24 hour hotline.
www.bhrc.co.uk   ☎ 020 7340 1616

Hostels London
Online reservations. Accredited member of The Federation of International Youth Travel Operators. Includes St. Christopher's Inns.
www.hostelslondon.net

International Booking Network (operated by International Youth Hostel Federation)
Bed price varies with age (up to 18 and 18+).
36 Carter Lane, EC4
www.hostelbooking.com   ☎ 020 7236 4965

London Bed & Breakfast Agency Ltd.
From £22 per person per night. Accommodation in private homes all over London.
71 Fellows Road, NW3
www.londonbb.com   ☎ 020 7586 2768

London Tourist Board
This website also has a database for accommodation listed as 'disabled accessible', places that accept Guide and Hearing dogs, self-catering, B&B and Halls of Residence.
www.visitlondon.com   ☎ 020 7932 2020

Major hotels

Listed below are contact details for some of the larger hotel chains plus the more exclusive hotels. There is also a selection of accommodation at lower price ranges. Note that prices can vary depending on special deals, time of booking, booking agency deals etc.
The following symbols give a guide to price ranges:

£ = under £80/room   £££ = £120 to £200
££ = £80 to £120   ££££ = £200+

◆ Selected hotels

Bedford
Pleasant hotel with 184 rooms. **From £**
Southampton Row, WC1   ☎ 020 7636 7822

Bloomsbury Park
Comfortable hotel with 95 rooms. **££**
126 Southampton Row, WC1   ☎ 020 7430 0434

Bloomsbury Thistle
A fine Edwardian hotel with 138 rooms. **From £**
Bloomsbury Way, WC1   ☎ 020 7242 5881

Bonnington
A pleasant hotel with excellent facilities for disabled guests. **£££**
92 Southampton Row, WC1   ☎ 020 7242 2828

Britannia
A luxurious Georgian hotel overlooking Grosvenor Square. **From ££**
Grosvenor Square, W1   ☎ 020 7629 9400

Brown's
The oldest hotel in London with a 'country house' atmosphere.
Afternoon tea here is world famous. Unique, exclusive and luxurious,
118 rooms. **££££**
Albemarle Street, W1   ☎ 020 7493 6020

Claridge's
Patronised by the rich and famous, this is a very exclusive hotel,
203 rooms. **££££**
Brook Street, W1   ☎ 020 7629 8860

Dolphin Square
An all-suite hotel set in lovely gardens near the Thames. **£££**
Chichester Street, SW1   ☎ 020 7834 3800

Dorchester
Overlooking Hyde Park, this stylish hotel has sumptuous rooms. **££££**
Park Lane, W1   ☎ 020 7629 8888

Durrants
Comfortable, friendly and traditionally English. Near Oxford Street. **£££**
George Street, W1   ☎ 020 7935 8131

Ibis
A modern 380 room hotel convenient for Euston. **£££**
3 Cardington Street, NW1   ☎ 020 7388 7777

Jurys, Islington
Modern hotel with 229 rooms. **From £**
60 Pentonville Road, N1   ☎ 020 7282 5500

London Ryan
Good hotel in central London with 211 rooms. **From ££**
10-42 King's Cross Road, WC1   ☎ 020 7278 2480

Mandeville
An Edwardian hotel with 166 rooms and modern facilities. **££ to £££**
Mandeville Place, W1   ☎ 020 7935 5599

Moat House, Sloane Square
An elegant 105 room hotel in fashionable Sloane Square. **££**
Sloane Square, SW1   ☎ 020 7896 9988

Ramada Plaza
Modern 11 storey hotel, 377 rooms. Opposite Lord's Cricket Ground. **£££**
18 Lodge Road, NW8   ☎ 020 7722 7722

Ritz
Luxury hotel with French elegance. All rooms are decorated in the Ritz colour schemes of blue, peach, pink and yellow. Traditional features and state of the art facilities. **££££**
150 Piccadilly, W1   ☎ 020 7493 8181

Savoy
Luxurious hotel. Very Art Deco with 154 rooms, some overlooking the Thames. In the heart of West End theatre land. **££££**
Strand, WC2   ☎ 020 7836 4343

Sherlock Holmes
Stunningly refurbished hotel with modern elegance and many luxurious facilities. **From ££**
108 Baker Street, W1   ☎ 020 7486 6161

Tavistock
Art Deco hotel overlooking the gardens of Tavistock Square. **From £**
Tavistock Square, WC1 ☎ 020 7636 8383

Waldorf
All 292 rooms in this distinctive luxury hotel are designed in an
Edwardian style. Impressive health and leisure suite. **££££**
Aldwych, WC2 ☎ 020 7836 2400

Westminster
Close to Paddington rail station but in a quiet garden square. Modern,
comfortable and friendly. 116 rooms. **££ to £££**
16 Leinster Square, W2 ☎ 020 7286 5294

◆ Hotel chains

Comfort Inns & Quality Hotels
Comfortable, good value hotels at convenient locations. **From £**
www.comfortinn.com ☎ 0800 44 44 44

Grange Hotels
New, luxury hotels all over central London with all the comforts you
would expect from top of the range accommodation. **££££**
www.grangehotels.com ☎ 020 7233 7888

Hilton Hotels
Top of the range luxury hotels. The Hilton Park Lane is the flagship of
the Hilton Group. Very modern, with 450 rooms on 28 storeys. **££££**
www.hilton.com ☎ 08705 90 90 90

Holiday Inns
Mid-range comfortable hotels. **From ££**
www.holidayinn.co.uk ☎ 0800 40 50 60

Marriott Hotels
Comfortable hotels at convenient locations. **£££**
www.marriott.com ☎ 020 7591 1500

Thistle Hotel chain
Mid-price range hotels all over London. **From ££**
www.thistlehotels.com ☎ 0870 333 9292

Travel Inns
Good, basic hotels aiming to provide everything you need for a good
night's sleep. **£**
www.travelinn.co.uk ☎ 0870 242 8000

Eating & Drinking

Restaurants

London is a haven for the gastronome, with food from every corner of the globe. Some restaurants are expensive, some are better than others and it is always wise to book. The list below does not include the excellent hotel restaurants, it is simply a very small selection from some of the better establishments dedicated to providing delicious cuisine. To book online, try www.timeout.com/london/restaurants

◆ African

Pasha
Cosy, atmospheric restaurant, large choice of traditional food.
1 Gloucester Road, SW7   ☎ 020 7589 7969

Calabash
Next to Covent Garden, this reasonably priced restaurant offers excellent food with vegetarian options.
The Africa Centre, 38 King Street, WC2   ☎ 020 7836 1976

◆ American

Christopher's
Good pre-theatre menu with friendly staff and pleasant ambience.
18 Wellington Street, WC2   ☎ 020 7240 4222

Black & Blue
High quality, fresh, simple food cooked well, especially the beef. Friendly staff and good value for money. No booking.
215-217 Kensington Church Street, W8   ☎ 020 7727 0004

Hard Rock Café
Good food and service, rock music and great atmosphere. Queues to get in but you can pre-book (but not for an exact time) on the website www.hardrock.com
150 Old Park Lane, W1   ☎ 020 7629 0382

◆ Belgian

Abbaye
Superb seafood, friendly staff, wide choice of Belgian beers.
55 Charterhouse Street, EC1   ☎ 020 7253 1612

◆ British

Alfred
Delicious modern and classic British food in uncluttered setting.
245 Shaftesbury Avenue, WC2 ☎ 020 7240 2566

The Oxo Tower Restaurant
Serves modern British food with lovely views over London.
Oxo Tower Wharf, Barge House Street, SE1 ☎ 020 7803 3888

40 Degrees at Veronica's
Food from every period of British history, starting with medieval.
3 Hereford Road, W2 ☎ 020 7229 5079

Rules
The oldest restaurant in London (1798). Traditional British food.
35 Maiden Lane, WC2 ☎ 020 7836 5314

◆ Chinese

Fung Shing
One of the best. Interesting speciality dishes and exceptional service.
15 Lisle Street, WC2 (Chinatown) ☎ 020 7437 1539

Tiger Lil's
Choose your own ingredients and have them cooked in front of you.
270 Upper Street, N1 ☎ 020 7226 1118

Choys
Attentive staff in this welcoming restaurant. Good choice of food.
172 Kings Road, SW3 ☎ 020 7352 0505

◆ French

Le Café du Marche
First class service and food, extensive wine list. Quiet jazz downstairs.
22 Charterhouse Square, EC1 ☎ 020 7608 1609

Pied à Terre
High standards in food and service. Good value set menu for lunch.
34 Charlotte Street, W1 ☎ 020 7636 1178

Mon Plaisir
Excellent French food at reasonable prices. Pre-theatre menu.
21 Monmouth Street, WC2 ☎ 020 7836 7243

◆ Greek

Andreas
Delicious Greek food with a warm and friendly atmosphere.
22 Charlotte Street, W1 ☎ 020 7580 8971

The Real Greek
Tasty 'untypical' Greek food with friendly service. All the wine is Greek.
14-15 Hoxton Market, N1 ☎ 020 7739 8212

◆ Hungarian

The Gay Hussar
Welcoming atmosphere and great Hungarian food.
2 Greek Street, W1 ☎ 020 7437 0973

◆ Indian

Rasa Samudra
Food from southern India, cooked well. Good vegetarian selection too.
5 Charlotte Street, W1 ☎ 020 7637 0222

Zaika
Excellent food recognised by the attainment of a Michelin star.
1 Kensington High Street, W8 ☎ 020 7795 6533

Masala Zone
Fresh, authentic Indian food with outstanding 'street food' dishes. Tribal art décor and friendly service. Good value.
9 Marshall Street, W1 ☎ 020 7287 9966

◆ Irish

ArdRi at the O'Conor Don
Homely dining with friendly service and traditional food.
88 Marylebone Lane, W1 ☎ 020 7935 9311

◆ Italian

Isolabella
High quality food and special service.
45-46 Red Lion Street, WC1 ☎ 020 7405 6830

Carluccio's Caffe Smithfield
Fresh, excellent food, wonderful ice cream. Very helpful staff.
12 West Smithfield, EC1 ☎ 020 7329 5904

Sapori
Good Italian food, often with a unique twist. Friendly service.
43 Drury Lane, WC2   ☎ 020 7836 8296

Zafferano
Imaginative Italian food in this well established restaurant. Excellent
wine list.
15 Lowndes Street, SW1   ☎ 020 7235 5800

◆ Japanese

Benihana (Soho)
Entertaining chefs cooking excellent food.
37 Sackville Street, W1   ☎ 020 7494 2525

Ikkyu
Wide range of fresh authentic food complementing the Sushi menu.
Friendly Japanese staff and relaxing atmosphere.
67a Tottenham Court Road, W1   ☎ 020 7636 9280

Ginnan
Just excellent Japanese food. Good value lunchtime menu.
1 Rosebery Court, Rosebery Avenue, EC1   ☎ 020 7278 0008

◆ Korean

Han Kang
Good selection of fresh, well-prepared food.
16 Hanway Street, W1   ☎ 020 7637 1985

◆ Mexican

Café Pacifico
First rate margaritas along with a lively atmosphere and friendly service.
5 Langley Street, WC2   ☎ 020 7379 7728

◆ Middle East

Sofra (Covent Garden)
Appetising food, excellent service, reasonable prices.
36 Tavistock Street, WC2   ☎ 020 7240 3773

Maroush
Open until the early hours, food and service are exemplary. Interesting
décor.
38 Beauchamp Place, SW3   ☎ 020 7581 5434

◆ Scandinavian

Lundums
Classic Danish fayre cooked to perfection. Elegant but relaxed atmosphere.
119 Old Brompton Road, SW7 ☎ 020 7373 7774

◆ Spanish

Meson Don Felipe
Well established restaurant serving great food (try the tapas) with a buzzing atmosphere.
53 The Cut, SE1 ☎ 020 7928 3237

La Rueda
Authentic Spanish food with dancing later.
102 Wigmore Street, W1 ☎ 020 7486 1718

◆ Thai

Nahm
Traditional Royal Thai cuisine in David Thompson's restaurant.
The Halkin, 5 Halkin Street, SW1 ☎ 020 7333 1234

Thai Terrace
Very good Thai food served in a friendly atmosphere.
14 Wrights Lane, W8 ☎ 020 7938 3585

Champor Champor
Small restaurant with excellent food and good service.
62 Weston Street, SE1 ☎ 020 7403 4600

◆ Vegetarian

Food For Thought
Small busy restaurant with good food in a homely atmosphere.
31 Neal Street, WC2 ☎ 020 7836 9072

The Nuthouse
Wholesome veggie food in a delightful atmosphere.
26 Kingly Street, W1 ☎ 020 7437 9471

Mildred's
Tasty food in generous portions. Caters for wheat and dairy allergies.
45 Lexington Street, W1 ☎ 020 7494 1634

Fast food

Fast food is available all over London. Chains include **KFC** (chicken), **Strada** (excellent pizza), **Wagamama** (Japanese), **Soup Works** (soup and noodles) and **Prêt-à-Manger** (sandwiches). For coffee and a snack, try chains such as **Costa Coffee** and **Starbucks**. Good individual places include **Bar Italia** in Soho, which provides coffee and a snack at almost any time, **Sweetings** in Queen Victoria Street (very old company serving excellent fish). **Clark & Sons** are an eel and pie shop in Exmouth Market and **Arkansas Café** is an American BBQ near Liverpool Street underground.

☺ If you have children with you, there are some admirable quick bite chains. Try **Ed's Diners'** (retro with milkshakes and burgers), **Café Rouge** (adult dining with kids portions and activity packs). **The Rainforest Café** in Soho has waterfalls, animated creatures, mist and exotic food, or **Planet Hollywood** 💳 has lots of entertainment. **Belgo Central** in Covent Garden serves sausage and mash with other children's favourites and under 12s can eat free. In Bloomsbury, **China House** is a good place for oriental food with children's portions and entertainment for them in the afternoons.

Afternoon tea

The very English tradition of afternoon tea can still be enjoyed in many establishments. The following offer the 'crème de la crème' of this institution.

Brown's Hotel
Like a country house, with a pianist and, in the colder months, a roaring fire. Booking recommended. Smart casual dress. Weekdays 3pm to 5.45pm, weekends from 2.30pm, cost around £23 per person.
Albemarle Street, W1   ☎ 020 7493 6020

Claridge's Hotel
Very smart and civilised. Tea, accompanied by music, served in the Reading Room. Booking recommended. Smart casual dress. From 3pm to 5.30pm, cost around £26 per person.
Brook Street, W1   ☎ 020 7629 8860

The Dorchester Hotel
Potted palms, sumptuous sofas and marble columns. Booking recommended. Smart casual dress. Afternoon tea (served 3pm to 6pm) costs around £23.50 per person and high tea (served 5pm to 8pm) costs £32.50 per person.
Park Lane, W1   ☎ 020 7629 8888

The Ritz Hotel
Tea served in the Palm Court amid chandeliers and potted palms.
Booking essential six weeks in advance. Smart casual dress. From 1.30pm
to 5.30pm, cost around £30 per person.
150 Piccadilly, W1   ☎ 020 7493 8181

Pubs & wine bars

◆ Wine bar or pub?

The alternative to the traditional English pub is a wine bar. Generally, it
will be part of a restaurant or bistro, perhaps with pavement tables,
and it will specialise in wines, light beers and lager. A pub has a totally
different ambience; open fires, quiet rooms in an old building, polished
brass and 'real ale' (made from a traditional recipe and hand-pulled
from barrels). The line between pubs and wine bars is becoming ever
more blurred, however, with the improvements in food being served in
pubs and heavier beers on tap in wine bars.
Opening hours vary but are generally 11am to 11pm and many London
pubs are closed on Sundays. Note that the age limit for buying or
consuming alcohol is 18 and you must be 14 or over to go in. Children
under 14 can be taken by an adult into a pub serving food.

◆ Wine bars

El Vino 30 New Bridge Street, EC4, **Carriages** 43 Buckingham Palace
Road, SW1, **Eatons** 1 Minster Pavement, Mincing Lane, EC3, **Cork and
Bottle** Cranbourne Street, Leicester Square, WC2, **Crusting Pipe** The
Market, Covent Garden, WC2, **Tappit Hen** William IV Street, Covent
Garden, WC2, **Cicada** St. John Street, EC1, **Fluid** Charterhouse Street,
EC1.

◆ Pubs

There are basically two types, chain and individual pubs. The former
include the Slug & Lettuce and J.D. Weatherspoons (who serve good
food and guest ales at bargain prices), the latter include 'traditional'
old pubs and those in newer re-vamped premises, often with a 'theme'.
Try some of the following 'traditional' pubs:

Anchor
Riverside pub with plenty of seating ouside.
Bankside, SE1   ☎ 020 7407 0741

Black Friar
Art nouveau outside, Edwardian inside with good beer.
174 Queen Victoria Street, EC4　　　　☎ 020 7236 5474

Bunch of Grapes
Victorian pub with finely engraved 'snob' screens which kept the well-to-do away from the 'riff-raff'.
207 Brompton Road, SW3　　　　☎ 020 7589 4944

Fox & Anchor
Huge English breakfasts at 7am and good beer in this Edwardian pub.
115 Charterhouse Street, EC1　　　　☎ 020 7253 5075

Lamb & Flag
This wooden framed building (one of London's last) was built in 1623 and serves real ale.
33 Rose Street, WC2　　　　☎ 020 7497 9504

Salisbury
Beautiful Victorian traditional pub.
90 St. Martin's Lane, WC2　　　　☎ 020 7836 5863

Spread Eagle
Right in the heart of Camden, a traditional pub serving real ales.
141 Albert Street, NW1　　　　☎ 020 7267 1410

The Hope
Real ales and sausage 'n' mash lunches.
15 Tottenham Street, W1　　　　☎ 020 7637 0896

The Sherlock Holmes
Classic London pub, cosy with lots of Sherlock Holmes memorabilia.
10 Northumberland Avenue, WC2　　　　☎ 020 7930 2644

◆ Less traditional but also excellent:

Freedom Brewing Company
A very successful microbrewery with whitewashed walls.
41 Earlham Street, WC2　　　　☎ 020 7240 0606

Mash
Space age décor with real ale brewed in its own microbrewery.
19-21 Great Portland Street, W1　　　　☎ 020 7637 5555

28

Shopping

Shopping areas & markets

The many diverse shopping areas in London each have their own character. To find what you want, it is essential to determine in which area you are most likely to find it.

◆ Shopping areas

New Bond Street, W1
Large, well-known exclusive designer fashion, plus antiques.

Old Bond Street, W1
Wall to wall jewellery shops including Tiffany's and Aspreys.

Knightsbridge, SW1
Haute couture shopping and expensive, unique, designer *objets d'art* and antiques.

Oxford Street, W1
Mainly leading high street department stores.

Regent Street, W1/SW1
More 'up market' department stores, smaller fashion shops, jewellery and china. Excellent for Christmas shopping when the illuminations are a sight in themselves.

Burlington Arcade, W1 (between Burlington Gardens & Piccadilly)
Famous, traditional London shops in a bygone setting. Uniformed guards make sure that shopping here is a calm and pleasant experience.

Carnaby Street, W1
Funky fashion, contemporary designer jewellery and anything trendy.

Charing Cross Road, WC2
Book shops galore. Foyle's (the biggest) down to small, specialist stores.

Denmark Street, WC2
A number of shops specialising in musical instruments.

Hatton Garden, EC1
The place for jewellery. Over 60 glittering shops where you can buy or commission stunning pieces. The home of De Beers.

Jermyn Street, SW1
Bespoke gentlemen's clothing.

Kings Road, SW3
Small, exclusive boutiques.

Savile Row, W1
World famous for its bespoke tailors, you can purchase hand-made suits and superior 'off the peg' versions.

St. James Street, SW1
Really interesting 'one off' shops selling hats, boots, cigars etc.

Tottenham Court Road, W1
Bargain electrical goods, mainly computers and hi-fi.

◆ Markets

There are hundreds of markets in London ranging from open-air craft markets to Sunday morning street markets selling clothes and general household goods. They can often be the place to seek out special items or unusual fashions.

Bermondsey Market
The largest antiques market in London. Fri from 5am.
Long Lane/Bermondsey Street, SE1

Borough Market
Gourmet food in abundance, from organic vegetables to hand-made cheeses and Morecambe Bay shrimps. Open from noon on Fri and 9am on Sat.
Southwark Street, SE1

Covent Garden Market
Wonderful original crafts. Open daily from 9am.
Covent Garden, WC2

Grays Antique Market
Over 80 dealers housed in one building. Open Mon to Fri from 10am.
58 Davies Street, W1

Leadenhall Market
Next to the amazing Lloyd's of London building designed by Richard Rogers, this food market sells traditional meats and fish along with specialist foods such as chocolate. Mon to Fri from 7am.
Whittington Avenue, EC3

Old Spitalfields Market
With over 200 stalls on a Sunday, selling everything from organic food
to jewellery, you can spend the day here. Open from 11am.
Commercial Street, E1

Petticoat Lane
Open Sun to Fri (best on Sun), from 9am, this market is famous for
clothes; be they genuine retro or last year's designer. Leather wear is a
speciality. Also bric-a-brac.
Middlesex Street, E1

Other well known markets outside the area of this guide include
Camden Markets, NW1, **Columbia Road Flower Market**, E2 and
Portobello Road, W11.

The big stores

There are several large stores in London where you can buy practically
anything. Others are slightly more specialised, but still offer a wide
choice of goods.

Debenhams
Fashions and homeware at competitive prices, plus much more.
334-348 Oxford Street, W1 ☎ 020 7580 3000
www.debenhams.com

Fenwick
Fashions for men and women on five floors. Also beauty products and a
beauty studio.
63 New Bond Street, W1 ☎ 020 7629 9161
www.fenwick.co.uk

Fortnum & Mason
Almost 300 years old, this famous old store still sells the best in food;
teas, hampers and confectionery now sit alongside fine porcelain, linens
and other quality wares.
181 Piccadilly, W1 ☎ 020 7734 8040
www.fortnumandmason.com

Hamleys ⏱
At 240 years old, this is still considered to be the best toyshop in the
world. Seven floors of toys, games and gifts. Toy demonstrations and
events going on all the time.
188-196 Regent Street, W1 ☎ 0870 333 2455
www.hamleys.co.uk

Harrods
Everything you would expect in a department store, plus a very famous food hall and 22 restaurants!
87-135 Brompton Road, SW1 ☎ 020 7730 1234
www.harrods.com

Harvey Nichols
Best known for its designer clothes, Harvey Nichols stocks some of the best of British, European, American and Far Eastern names.
109-125 Knightsbridge, SW1 ☎ 020 7235 5000
www.harveynichols.com

John Lewis
Competitive pricing and a huge range of goods makes a visit to one of London's largest department stores well worthwhile.
Oxford Street, W1 ☎ 020 7629 7711
www.johnlewis.com

Liberty
This purpose built store sells beautiful fabrics influenced by the Arts and Crafts movement. Clothes, bedlinens, furnishings and gifts.
210 Regent Street, W1 ☎ 020 7734 1234
www.liberty.co.uk

Lillywhites
Everything you could want for every type of sport under one roof.
24-36 Regent Street, SW1 ☎ 020 7930 3181
www.lillywhites.co.uk

Marks & Spencer
This flagship store not only has a wide selection of clothes, homewares and food but it also has a bureau de change and instant cash refunds for tax-free eligible customers.
Marble Arch, W1 ☎ 020 7935 7954
www.marksandspencer.com

Selfridges
Six floors of everything, including fashion, household goods and a famous food hall and perfumery.
Oxford Street, W1 ☎ 020 7629 1234
www.selfridges.co.uk

Virgin Megastore
Huge store selling music in all formats, computer games and videos.
14-19 Oxford Street, W1 ☎ 020 7631 1234
www.virginmega.co.uk

Specialist shops

London is an international centre for art, fashion, antiques and collectors' items. Many shops have specialised in certain goods and have become world-famous names. The list below represents only a selection of some of the best shops in each category.

◆ Antiques

Baroque & Roll, 291 Lillie Road, SW6. Antiques, old and not so old.
David Aaron, 22 Berkeley Square, W1. Antiques and rare carpets.
Eaton Gallery, 34 Duke Street, SW1. Oil paintings, watercolours and drawings.
Map World, 25 Burlington Arcade, W1. Antique maps and atlases.
Marks Antiques, 49 Curzon Street, W1. Antique silver from great designers.

◆ Auctioneers

Bonham's, 101 New Bond Street, W1. Flagship London saleroom for fine art and antiques.
Christie's, 8 King Street, SW1. Fine art auctioneers since 1766.
Sotheby's, 34-35 New Bond Street, W1. World famous auction house for paintings, ceramics, glass, furniture, jewellery and books.

◆ Books

European Bookshop, 5 Warwick Street, W1. Wide selection of books and periodicals in many European languages.
Foyles, 113-119 Charing Cross Road, WC2. The biggest independent bookshop.
Maggs Brothers, 50 Berkeley Square, W1. Antique and rare books.
Murder One, 71-73 Charing Cross Road, WC2. Books of 'orrible' murder stories, both real life and fiction.
Stanford's, 12-14 Long Acre, WC2. Books on travel and all the maps you could need.
Ulysses, 40 Museum Street, WC1. First editions from the 20th century.
Waterstones, 203-206 Piccadilly, W1. One of the largest general bookstores in London.

◆ China, glass & silver

London Silver Vaults, 53-64 Chancery Lane, WC2. Over 30 underground shops selling antique and modern silver.
Thomas Goode, South Audley Street, W1. Exclusive china, glass and silver.

◆ Clothes

Burberry, 18-22 Haymarket, SW1. Famous trenchcoats plus lots more.
Captain Watts, 7 Dover Street, W1. Nautical oilskins and jumpers.
Jean Muir, 22 Bruton Street W1. Elegant designer clothes.
Jean-Paul Gaultier, 171-175 Draycott Avenue, SW3. Designer clothes.
Pringle, New Bond Street, W1. Luxury knitwear.
Rigby & Peller, 22 Conduit Street, W1. Lingerie made to measure.

◆ Jewellery

Angela Hale, 5 Royal Arcade, Bond Street. Art Deco and 50s style jewellery.
Asprey, New Bond Street, W1. The Crown Jewellers, making and selling exquisite pieces.
Manquette, 40 Gordon Place, W8. Precious and semi precious gems in gold and silver.
N. Bloom & Son, Piccadilly Arcade W1. Old jewellery, plus classic old watches.
The Great Frog, 10 Ganton Street, W1. Gothic-style pieces.
Tiffany's, 25 Old Bond Street, W1. THE jewellers!

◆ Music

Ray's Jazz, 180 Shaftesbury Avenue, WC2. Jazz music CDs etc.
Stern's, 293 Euston Road, NW1. African music of all types.

◆ Perfume

Floris, 89 Jermyn Street, SW1. Classic Floris fragrances in a really beautiful shop.
Jo Malone, 150 Sloane Street, SW1. Fragrance combining, facials, hand and arm massage.

◆ One offs

Anything Left-Handed, 57 Brewer Street, W1. Kitchen utensils, tools, scissors and much more, all designed for the left-handed.
Falkiner Fine Papers, 76 Southampton Row, WC1. Decorative and hand-made paper for wrapping or writing.
James Smith & Sons, 53 New Oxford Street, W1. Umbrellas and walking sticks from the oldest shop of its kind in Europe!
Lock's, St. James Street, SW1. A wide range of hats for men and women.
Lulu Guinness, 3 Ellis Street, SW1. Unique handbags.
Paxton and Whitfield, 93 Jermyn Street, SW1. Cheeses, cheeses and more cheeses!
Tea House, Covent Garden. Huge selection of teas and tea requisites.

Entertainment

London hosts world-class events and exhibitions. It also boasts a thriving night life. See the latest blockbuster at one of the many cinemas or a show at one of the famous West End theatres. Then there's a vast choice of venues from the live music, club and comedy scene.

Booking tickets

Lists of current cinema, theatre, dance, music and comedy performances can be found in national newspapers, the *Evening Standard* newspaper and *Time Out* magazine. There is also the *Official London Theatre Guide* from tourist information centres. When booking, ask to see a seating plan (is the view restricted?), if necessary ask for details on disabled access and do not buy from people on the street.

◆ Box Offices

If you call in at a theatre and buy in person, there is usually no booking fee, if you book by telephone, there might be. The box office is usually open from 10am until just after the start of the performance. On the day, you may be fortunate and get a returned ticket or standby ticket.

◆ Ticket booth, Leicester Square

This is in the clocktower building and sells half price tickets on the day of the performance. Seat positions cannot be specified. The Society of London Theatre's only official booth.

◆ Ticket agencies

The choice is vast, and most are genuine. Make sure they are members of an organisation called STAR. There is always a booking fee and sometimes a transaction fee. Find out the true price of the ticket from the theatre first, the booking fee should be no more than 25% of this. Some members of STAR are **Ticketmaster** www.ticketmaster.co.uk, **First Call** ☎ 0870 906 3838 www.firstcalltickets.com, or in person at Virgin Megastores in Oxford Street, Piccadilly Circus and Camden High Street.

◆ Online

Buy online from the theatre website.

Cinemas

◆ Leicester Square cinemas showing the latest films

Many of the larger cinemas are centred on Leicester Square, WC2. They screen the latest releases and are the venues for glitzy film premieres.

Odeon	☎ 0870 5050007
Odeon West End	☎ 0870 5050007
UCI Empire	☎ 0870 0102030
UGC Trocadero	☎ 0870 9070716
Warner West End	☎ 0870 2406020

◆ Other cinemas showing the latest films

Odeon Marble Arch
10 Edgware Road, W2 ☎ 0870 5050007

Odeon Tottenham Court Road
Tottenham Court Road, W1 ☎ 0870 5050007

◆ Independents

Barbican
Latest films, independent and arthouse.
Silk Street, EC2 ☎ 020 7382 7000

Ciné Lumière
French, European and world films with English subtitles.
17 Queensberry Place, SW7 ☎ 020 7073 1350

Curzon, Soho
Mostly arthouse and independent films.
Shaftesbury Avenue, W1 ☎ 020 7734 2255

IMAX
The UK's biggest cinema screen. 2D and 3D films.
1 Charlie Chaplin Walk, SE1 ☎ 020 7902 1234

National Film Theatre
Three screens showing everything from blockbusters to old classics.
South Bank, SE1 ☎ 020 7928 3232

Prince Charles
Classic, recent and cult films. Also Sing-a-long-a Sound of Music nights.
Leicester Place, WC2 ☎ 020 7494 3654

Theatres

The tradition of live theatre in London has flourished for more than four centuries. Today a wide range of productions are available, offering something for everyone.

◆ Theatres with backstage tours

Royal National ♿
Famous for its high standards, this repertory theatre has three auditoriums (the Olivier, Lyttelton and Cottesloe) which stage classics, new plays and musicals. Parking, restaurants, bookshop.
South Bank, SE1 ☎ 020 7452 3000
www.nationaltheatre.org.uk ☎ 020 7452 3600 (backstage tours)

Barbican ♿
Purpose-built for the Royal Shakespeare Company. The theatre has a main auditorium for large scale productions and there is the Pit, a smaller studio for new works.
Silk Street, EC2 ☎ 020 7638 8891
www.barbican.org.uk ☎ 020 7628 3351 (backstage tours)

Duke of York ♿
Peter Pan first appeared here! Smaller theatre showing West End plays.
St. Martin's Lane, WC2 ☎ 020 7369 1791
☎ 020 7369 1771 (backstage tours)

London Palladium ♿
Large theatre, famous for variety shows.
Argyll Street, W1 ☎ 020 7494 5020

Shakespeare's Globe 📷
Reconstruction of the original which was built nearby in 1599. No mod cons, as close as you can get to a 16th century performance. Also largest exhibition in the world about 'the Bard'.
21 New Globe Walk, Bankside, SE1 ☎ 020 7401 9919
www.shakespeares-globe.org

Theatre Royal, Drury Lane ♿
Destroyed by fire several times, the oldest playhouse in the world has survived to stage the best plays and musicals.
Catherine Street, WC2 ☎ 020 7494 5000

Theatre Royal, Haymarket ♿
Grade I listed building showing excellent plays.
Haymarket, SW1 ☎ 020 7930 8800

◆ Other mainstream theatres

Adelphi ♿ Strand, WC2	☎ 020 7344 0055
Albery ♿ St. Martin's Lane, WC2	☎ 020 7369 1740
Aldwych ♿ Aldwych, WC2	☎ 0870 4000 805
Apollo Shaftesbury Avenue, W1	☎ 020 7494 5070
Apollo Victoria ♿ Wilton Road, SW1	☎ 020 7834 6318
Criterion ♿ Piccadilly Circus, W1	☎ 020 7413 1437
Dominion ♿ Tottenham Court Road, W1	☎ 0870 6077400
Duchess Catherine Street, WC2	☎ 020 7494 5075
Fortune Russell Street, WC2	☎ 020 7369 1737
Garrick ♿ Charing Cross Road, WC2	☎ 020 7494 5080
Gielgud ♿ Shaftesbury Avenue, W1	☎ 020 7494 5065
Her Majesty's ♿ Haymarket, SW1	☎ 020 7494 5400
Lyric ♿ Shaftesbury Avenue, W1	☎ 020 7494 5045
New London ♿ Drury Lane, WC2	☎ 020 7404 4079
Old Vic ♿ Waterloo Road, SE1	☎ 020 7369 1722
Palace ♿ Shaftesbury Avenue, W1	☎ 020 7434 0909
Phoenix ♿ Charing Cross Road, WC2	☎ 020 7369 1733
Piccadilly ♿ Denman Street, W1	☎ 020 7369 1734
Playhouse ♿ Northumberland Avenue, WC2	☎ 020 7839 4401
Prince Edward ♿ Old Compton Street, W1	☎ 020 7447 5400
Prince of Wales Coventry Street, W1	☎ 020 7839 5972
Queen's ♿ Shaftesbury Avenue, W1	☎ 020 7494 5041
Royal Court ♿ Sloane Square, SW1	☎ 020 7565 5000
St. Martin's ♿ West Street, WC2	☎ 020 7836 1443
Savoy ♿ Strand, WC2	☎ 020 7836 8888
Shaftesbury ♿ Shaftesbury Avenue, W1	☎ 020 7379 5399
Vaudeville Strand, WC2	☎ 0870 890 0511
Victoria Palace ♿ Victoria Street, SW1	☎ 020 7834 1317
Whitehall 14 Whitehall, SW1	☎ 020 7369 1735
Wyndham's Charing Cross Road, WC2	☎ 020 7369 1736

◆ Fringe theatres

Bloomsbury 15 Gordon Street, WC1	☎ 020 7388 8822
Cochrane Southampton Row, WC1	☎ 020 7242 7040
Jermyn Street 16b Jermyn Street, SW1	☎ 020 7287 2875
Southwark Playhouse 62 Southwark Bridge Road, SE1	☎ 020 7620 3494
Union 204 Union Street, SE1	☎ 020 7261 9876

◆ Open-air theatre

World-class performances from June to September in the beautiful setting of Regent's Park, NW1. ♿
www.openairtheatre.org ☎ 020 7486 2431

Exhibition halls

Earls Court Exhibition Centre &
Hosts many large, high profile shows.
Old Brompton Road, SW5   ☎ 020 7385 1200
www.eco.co.uk

Royal Horticultural Halls (Lawrence Hall & Lindley Hall) &
As well as hosting the famous flower shows, there are also antique
fairs, wine tasting, record fairs and many other events.
80 Vincent Square, SW1   ☎ 020 7828 4125
www.horticultural-halls.co.uk

Other major London exhibition centres outside the area of this guide:
ExCeL, Mace Gateway, E16
www.excel-london.co.uk   ☎ 020 7069 5000
Olympia, Hammersmith Road, W14 &
www.eco.co.uk   ☎ 020 7385 1200

Concert halls

Royal Festival Hall &
This modern hall, home of the London Philharmonic Orchestra hosts
classical, jazz and contemporary music. The **Queen Elizabeth Hall**
(chamber music, small orchestral works) and **Purcell Room** (chamber
music and solo concerts) share the same site.
Belvedere Road, SE1   ☎ 020 7960 4242
www.rfh.org.uk

Royal Albert Hall &
Hosts everything from the 'Proms' concerts to tennis tournaments.
Kensington Gore, SW7   ☎ 020 7589 8212
www.royalalberthall.com

St. John's Concert Hall &
Classical music from symphony orchestras, choirs and solo performers.
Smith Square, SW1   ☎ 020 7222 1061
www.sjss.org.uk

Wigmore Hall &
Major international artists and musicians making their London debut.
36 Wigmore Street, W1   ☎ 020 7935 2141
www.wigmore-hall.org.uk

Opera & dance

Several venues in central London play host to leading national and international ballet, dance and opera companies.

London Coliseum &
The home of the English National Opera, all performances are sung in English. Ballet and contemporary dance share the venue. Backstage tours available.
St. Martin's Lane, WC2 ☎ 020 7632 8300
www.eno.org

The Place &
Experimental and contemporary dance performances. Visitors welcome and you can even have a go yourself!
17 Duke's Road, WC1 ☎ 020 7387 0161
www.theplace.org.uk

Royal Opera House &
Home to the Royal Ballet and the Royal Opera. Backstage tours available.
Covent Garden, WC2 ☎ 020 7304 4000
www.royalopera.org ☎ 020 7212 9123 (disabled person's helpline)

Sadler's Wells &
The three theatres in this building stage international dance, opera and musicals. Backstage tours available.
Rosebery Avenue, EC1 ☎ 020 7863 8000
www.sadlers-wells.com

Live music venues

Live music venues often overlap with nightclubs to use the building more economically, so you can sometimes stay in the same place after a band has finished and dance the night away! The only way to really find out what is happening after dark is to buy *Time Out* magazine or the *Evening Standard* newspaper. To see a live band in a pub might cost as little as £5 but expect to pay £50 or more for someone really famous.

Astoria - Rock 'n' roll plus
For the last twelve years, the Astoria has hosted gigs, concerts and club nights featuring big acts such as Oasis, Eminem and U2 as well as 'alternative' bands. Originally a pickle factory!
157 Charing Cross Road, WC2 ☎ 020 7344 0044

Roadhouse - Blues/Rock 'n' roll
Retro American style music and food. Bands play from 11pm (9pm Sat).
Sun free all evening.
35 The Piazza, WC2 ☎ 020 7395 5800

Ronnie Scott's - Jazz club
Originally established in 1959 in Gerard Street, this club features the
crème de la crème of jazz bands, along with other artists that 'fit the
atmosphere' but aren't necessarily jazz artists. 3 bars and an *à la carte*
menu complete your evening.
47 Frith Street, W1 ☎ 020 7439 0747

◆ **Other rock & pop**

Mean Fiddler, 157 Charing Cross Road, WC2 ☎ 020 7434 9592
Limelight, 136 Shaftesbury Avenue, WC2 ☎ 020 7434 0572
Rock Garden, 6-7 The Piazza, WC2 ☎ 020 7836 4052

◆ **Other Jazz**

100 Club, 100 Oxford Street, W1 ☎ 020 7636 0933
Jazz café, 5 Parkway, NW1 ☎ 020 7916 6060

◆ **Major venues further out**

Brixton Academy, 211 Stockwell Road, SW9 ☎ 020 7771 2000
Forum, 9-17 Highgate Road, NW5 ☎ 020 7284 1001
Hammersmith Apollo, Queen Caroline Street, W6 ☎ 0870 606 3400
London Arena, Isle of Dogs, E14 ☎ 020 7538 1212
Wembley Arena, Empire Way, Wembley, HA9 ☎ 0870 840 1111

Comedy clubs

Amused Moose Soho, Barcode, 3-4 Archer Street, W1 ☎ 020 8341 1341
Chuckle Club, London School of Economics, Houghton Street, WC2
☎ 020 7476 1672
Comedy at Soho Ho, Crown & Two Chairmen pub, 31 Dean Street, W1
☎ 020 8341 1341
Comedy Café, 66 Rivington Street, EC2 ☎ 020 7739 5706
Comedy Spot, 29 Maiden Lane, WC2 ☎ 020 7379 5900
Comedy Store, 1a Oxendon Street, SW1 ☎ 020 7344 0234
Jongleurs Camden Lock, 38 Middle Yard, NW1 ☎ 020 7428 5929

Clubs & discos

The clubbing scene in London changes nightly, so look at *Time Out* and choose your favourite style. Better known venues include:

Bar Rumba
Different music every night with discount early on. Food available too.
36 Shaftesbury Avenue, W1   ☎ 020 7287 2715

Hippodrome
One of the 'safer' venues it's also one of the largest in the world.
Cranbourn Street, WC2   ☎ 020 7437 4311

Ministry of Sound
Big name DJs. Home of house music.
103 Gaunt Street, SE1   ☎ 020 7378 6528

Stringfellows
Probably the best known. Touristy, expensive disco.
16 Upper St. Martin's Lane, WC2   ☎ 020 7240 5534

Velvet Room
Great DJs. Wide range of music.
143 Charing Cross Road, WC2   ☎ 020 7439 4655

Others include: **Café de Paris**, 3 Coventry Street, W1, **Equinox**, Leicester Square, WC2, **Gardening Club**, Covent Garden, WC2, **PoNaNa**, 230 Shepherd's Bush Road, W6, **Propaganda**, 201 Wardour Street, W1, **Borderline**, Tottenham Court Road, W1, **Emporium**, Oxford Circus, W1, **Legends**, Piccadilly Circus, W1.

Casinos

You need to be a member of a casino to gamble, so if you want to try the tables, you need to join, usually 48 hours beforehand. Some casinos are listed below.

Grosvenor Casinos own six venues in London, and you can join online. Contact ☎ 0800 0853 594 www.rank.com. **London Clubs International** also owns six casinos, contact ☎ 020 7518 0000 www.clublci.com. For **Gala Casinos**, contact www.galacasinos.co.uk.

Places to visit

Royal London

Over hundreds of years, the British Royal Family has left its mark on the capital city. There are palaces, memorials, pageantry and shops by Royal Appointment. Many ceremonies can be seen throughout the year (see 'When to visit') and many buildings are open to the public.

Banqueting House
The only surviving part of the Palace of Whitehall where Charles I was executed. Unique Rubens painting on the ceiling.
Mon to Sat 10am to 5pm. Adults £4, with concessions.
Whitehall, SW1   Information line ☎ 0870 751 5178.

Buckingham Palace
Built in 1705, this is the official London residence of the Queen. The 19 state rooms including the Throne Room, Ballroom and Picture Gallery and 42 acres of gardens are open to visitors during August and September. Treasures which can be seen include paintings by artists such as Rembrandt and superb examples of English and French furniture.
9.30am to 4.15pm. Timed ticket system. Adult £12, with concessions.
St. James's Park, SW1   Credit card booking ☎ 020 7321 2233

Kensington Palace
Home to the late Princess of Wales and other members of the Royal Family. The State Apartments, housing some of the Royal Collection and the Royal Ceremonial Dress Collection (which displays gowns dating from the 18th century) are open to the public.
Open mid March to mid October, daily from 10am to 6pm.
Adult £10.20, with concessions.
Kensington Gardens, W8   Credit card booking ☎ 0870 751 5180

The Queen's Gallery
The gallery is part of Buckingham Palace and has a changing exhibition of priceless items from the Royal Collection.
Open daily from 10am to 5.30pm. Adult £6.50, with concessions.
                Credit card booking ☎ 020 7321 2233

The Royal Mews
A working stable with beautiful horses and a permanent display of State carriages and cars.
Open 1 March to 31 October, 11am to 4pm (last admission 3.15pm), longer during August and September. Adult £5, with concessions.
                Credit card booking ☎ 020 7321 2233

Tower of London ⏱ 💼

Dating from 1066, this wonderfully preserved medieval fortress has served many functions, from a residence for Royalty to a safe for the Crown Jewels. The collection includes the famous Koh-i-Noor diamond and the Imperial State Crown with its 317-carat diamond. The Yeomen Warders or Beefeaters give guided tours, dressed in their ancient livery, or you can explore the Tower independently.

Open March to October, Mon to Sat 9am to 5pm (Sun from 10am). Winter Tue to Sat 9am to 4pm, Sun to Mon 10am to 4pm. Adults £12, with concessions.

Tower Hill, EC3

Credit card booking ☎ 0870 756 7070
Information line ☎ 020 7488 5694

Museums & galleries

London's national museums and galleries contain some of the richest collections in the world and are full of surprising treasures. They range from the vast British Museum to more recent and specialist additions, many of which incorporate interactive displays and exhibits.

◆ Museums

British Museum 💼 ♿

Founded in 1753, this is the oldest public museum in the world. It has almost 100 galleries, housing objects from all over the globe. The central courtyard has a modern glass and steel roof covering galleries, a reading room and a restaurant.

Opening hours vary for different areas. Phone for details. Guide and companion dogs welcome. Free.

Great Russell Street, WC1
www.thebritishmuseum.ac.uk

☎ 020 7323 8299 (Info desk)
☎ 020 7323 8181 (Box office)

Bank of England Museum

An interesting insight into the role of finance from the foundation of the bank in 1694. Besides displays of gold and banknotes, there are interactive exhibitions.

Open Mon to Fri. Free.

Threadneedle Street, EC2
www.bankofengland.co.uk

☎ 020 7601 3985
☎ 020 7601 5545 (disabled helpline)

Britain at War ♿

What life was really like for ordinary people in London during the Blitz of World War II. Sights, sounds and special effects recreate the terrifying atmosphere.

Open daily from 10am. Adult £7.50, with concessions.

64-66 Tooley Street, SE1
www.britainatwar.co.uk

☎ 020 7403 3171

Clink Prison Museum
Scenes showing the gruesome conditions in the prison.
Open daily. Adult £4, with concessions.
Soho Wharf, 1 Clink Street, SE1   ☎ 020 7403 6515
www.clink.co.uk

Design Museum ♿
Covering the last century of design, you can see everything from a Coke
bottle to an Austin mini car. Also glimpses of futuristic prototypes.
Open daily. Adults £6, with concessions.
28 Shad Thames, SE1   ☎ 020 7940 8790
www.designmuseum.org

Golden Hinde ⏰
A full size working reconstruction of Drake's 16th century galleon.
Open daily. Various workshops available. Self-guided tour, adults £2.75,
with concessions. Guided tour, adults £3.50, with concessions.
St. Mary Overie Dock, Cathedral Street, SE1   ☎ 0870 011 8700
www.goldenhinde.co.uk

HMS Belfast ⏰ 📷 ♿
World War II battleship on which you can explore all nine decks.
Open daily from 10am. Children under 16 must be accompanied by an
adult. Adult £5.80, with concessions. Children under 16 free.
Morgan's Lane, Tooley Street, SE1   ☎ 020 7940 6300
www.iwm.org.uk/belfast   ☎ 020 7940 6323 (disabled helpline)

Imperial War Museum
The national museum of war history. Open daily. Free.
Lambeth Road, SE1   ☎ 020 7416 5320
www.iwm.org.uk/lambeth

London Dungeon ⏰ 📷
Not recommended for the nervous, this is a really scary experience with
displays of horrific punishments and torture. The latest technology
enables you to wander round the streets at the time of Jack the Ripper.
Open daily from 9.30am. Under 15s must be accompanied by an adult.
Adults £11.50, with concessions.
28/34 Tooley Street, SE1   ☎ 020 7403 7221
www.dungeons.co.uk

London Transport Museum ⏰ 📷
200 years of vehicles and memorabilia on display. Keep the children
happy in 'KidZone', with its interactive exhibitions.
Open daily. Adults £5.95, under 16's free.
Covent Garden Piazza, WC2   ☎ 020 7379 6344
www.ltmuseum.co.uk

Madame Tussaud's ⏱ ♿
Amazingly lifelike and life-size waxwork figures of villains and heroes from the past and present. Includes royalty, pop stars, film stars, statesmen and astronauts.
Open daily from 9am. Adults from £16.95 (prices vary according to date and time), includes entry to The Planetarium.
Marylebone Road, NW1   ☎ 0870 400 3000
www.madame-tussauds.com

Museum of London
The fascinating story of London's social history, from prehistoric times to the present day, told through exhibitions and 'hands on' displays.
Open daily. Free.
London Wall, EC2   ☎ 020 7600 3699
www.museum-london.org.uk

Natural History Museum ⏱ ♿
Hundreds of excellent interactive exhibits covering all aspects of the natural world, from earthquakes to dinosaurs and the latest discoveries.
Open daily. Children under 12 must be accompanied by an adult. Free.
Cromwell Road, SW7   ☎ 020 7942 5000 (weekdays)
www.nhm.ac.uk   ☎ 020 7942 5011 (weekends)

Old Operating Theatre Museum 🎫
The oldest surviving operating theatre in Britain, dating from 1822, restored to recreate the gruesome story of surgery before anaesthetics.
Open daily from 10.30am. Adults £4, with concessions.
St. Thomas's Church, St. Thomas Street, SE1   ☎ 020 7955 4791
www.thegarret.org.uk

Planetarium ⏱ ♿
The 30 minute 3D show takes you on a voyage of discovery into the solar system and beyond.
Open daily, several shows per day. Disabled access but phone first.
Adults from £16.95 (prices vary according to date and time), includes entry to Madame Tussaud's.
Marylebone Road, NW1   ☎ 0870 400 3000
www.london-planetarium.com

Science Museum ⏱ ♿
Seven floors housing stunning examples of the world's scientific inventions, covering everything from steam power to space exploration.
Open daily. Free. Charges for IMAX, Virtual Voyager, simulator and some special exhibitions.
Exhibition Road, SW7   ☎ 020 7942 4446 (disabled helpline)
www.sciencemuseum.org.uk   ☎ 0870 870 4771

Victoria & Albert Museum
A superb museum of Decorative Arts, with jewellery, textiles, furniture and much more, some dating from 3000 BC. The last Friday of each month has a catwalk show staging the latest fashions.
Open daily, late on Wednesdays and the last Friday of each month. Free.
Cromwell Road, SW7   ☎ 020 7942 2000
www.vam.ac.uk   ☎ 0870 442 0809 (24 hour recorded information)

Vinopolis
Everything you could want to know about wine. Tours and wine tasting.
Open daily from 12pm. Late on Mon, Fri and Sat. Some exceptions, so phone first. Children allowed but no person under 18 allowed alcohol.
Adults £11.50, with concessions.
1 Bank End, SE1   ☎ 0870 241 4040
www.vinopolis.co.uk   ☎ 0870 4444 777 (advance booking)

◆ Galleries

Courtauld Institute Galleries
Paintings, sculpture and other works of art, including Old Master, Impressionist and Post Impressionist paintings.
Open daily. Adults £5 with concessions, free on Mondays 10am to 2pm.
Somerset House, Strand, WC2   ☎ 020 7848 2589
www.courtauld.ac.uk   ☎ 020 7848 2526 (recorded)

National Gallery
A 'must' for any art lover, this gallery houses Western European paintings from the mid-1200s to 1900, including Van Gogh, Rembrandt and Botticelli. Permanent and changing exhibitions.
Open daily, late on Wednesdays. Free.
Trafalgar Square, WC2   ☎ 020 7747 2885
www.nationalgallery.org.uk

National Portrait Gallery
Likenesses of the famous and infamous, from the early 1600s painting of Shakespeare to modern icons from the sport and music worlds.
Open daily, late on Thur and Fri. Free, except some special exhibitions.
St. Martin's Place, WC2   ☎ 020 7306 0055
www.npg.org.uk   ☎ 020 7312 2463 (recorded)

Royal Academy of Arts
A unique collection of mainly British art from the 1700s to the present.
Open daily, late on Fridays. Charges vary for each exhibition.
Burlington House, Piccadilly, W1   ☎ 020 7300 8000
   ☎ 020 7300 5760/1 (recorded)

Saatchi Gallery ♿
Modern and sometimes controversial art, including works by Damien Hirst and Jenny Saville. The focus is to promote young British artists.
Open daily, late on Fri and Sat. Adults £8.50, with concessions.
County Hall, Westminster Bridge, SE1 ☎ 020 7823 2363
www.saatchi-gallery.co.uk ☎ 0870 1660 278 (advance tickets)

Tate Britain ♿
The best of British art from 1500 to the present. See works by artists from Constable to Hockney, Gainsborough to Turner.
Open daily, late on Wed. Free, donations welcome.
Millbank, SW1 ☎ 020 7887 8000
☎ 020 7887 8008 (recorded)
www.tate.org.uk ☎ 020 7887 8888 (disabled helpline)

Tate Modern ♿
Housed in the huge airy building that was the Bankside Power Station, are stunning masterpieces from 1900 to the present. Permanent and changing exhibitions feature Dali, Picasso and Warhol, as well as works by the latest contemporary artists.
Open daily, late on Fri and Sat. Free, donations welcome.
Bankside, SE1 ☎ 020 7887 8000
☎ 020 7887 8008 (recorded)
www.tate.org.uk ☎ 020 7887 8888 (disabled helpline)

Places of worship

Bevis Marks Synagogue
Built in 1700, this is Britain's oldest surviving synagogue.
Heneage Lane, EC3 ☎ 020 7626 1274

London Central Mosque
The centre for London's Muslims. Stunning 75ft (25m) high dome.
Regent's Park, NW8

St. Bartholomew-the-Great Church
One of London's oldest churches, dating from the early 1100s. Wonderful architecture and the setting for several films including *Shakespeare in Love* and *Four Weddings and a Funeral*.
Open Tue to Sun from 8.30am (Sat from 10.30am). Tours available, phone first. Free.
Cloth Fair, EC1 ☎ 020 7606 5171
www.greatstbarts.com

St. Clement Danes Church
First built by the Danes in the 9th century and rebuilt many times since. The nursery rhyme 'Oranges and Lemons' refers to these bells. Free.
Strand, WC2

St. Mary-le-Bow church
True Cockneys are born within the sound of the bells; Dick Whittington is said to have heard them too. Free.
Cheapside, EC2

St. Paul's Cathedral
This is probably Sir Christopher Wren's most famous building. Rising from the ashes of the Great Fire of London, it was completed in 1710. The magnificent dome affords superb views over London, as well as containing the famous 'whispering gallery'.
Open Mon to Sat from 8.30am. Services may close all or part of the building, phone first. Adults £6, with concessions. Guided tours extra.
Ludgate Hill, EC4 ☎ 020 7236 4128
www.stpauls.co.uk ☎ 020 7246 8319 (disabled access)

Southwark Cathedral
The present cathedral dates from the early 1200s. The tower has a superb view across the Thames, as shown in Hollar's famous drawing 'Long View of London'. A state of the art exhibition allows you to see this view, along with many of the artefacts recently discovered.
Open daily from 10am (11am Sun). Adults £3, with concessions.
Borough High Street, SE1 ☎ 020 7367 6734
www.dswark.org

Westminster Abbey
Housing the famous Coronation Chair, this building has seen the crowning of every new monarch (except two) since its foundation in 1065. The tomb of the Unknown Warrior resides here, representing all the fallen of World War I. Many poets are buried in 'Poets' Corner'.
Open Mon to Sat from 9.30am. Special services may close all or part of the building, phone first. Cloisters open daily from 8am. Garden open Tue, Wed and Thur from 10am. Adults £6, with concessions. Garden and cloisters free. Free to wheelchair users.
Broad Sanctuary, SW1 ☎ 020 7654 4900
www.westminster-abbey.org

Westminster Cathedral
This Cathedral is the headquarters of the Catholic Church in Britain. It is a Byzantine style building, built only a century ago and has the widest nave in England. Beautiful mosaics can be seen on the walls and floors.
Ashley Place, SW1 ☎ 020 7798 9055
www.westminstercathedral.org.uk

Monuments, statues & other landmarks

◆ Monuments & statues

Admiralty Arch, The Mall
Unique memorial to Queen Victoria built in 1910, it has three identical arches with wrought iron gates.

Albert Memorial, Kensington Gardens
Magnificent Gothic memorial to the husband of Queen Victoria. 175ft (53.3m) high, it holds a statue of Prince Albert who died in 1861.

Alfred the Great, Trinity Square
Dating from the 14th century this is the oldest statue in London. It depicts one of the greatest Kings of England.

Big Ben (St. Stephen's Tower), Parliament Square
The famous four-faced clock (the largest in Britain) sits in the 320ft (106m) St. Stephen's Tower which is part of the Houses of Parliament. The name 'Big Ben' refers to the 14 tonne bell. Not open to the public.

Boadicea (Boudicca), Victoria Embankment
An imposing statue of the famous British Queen and her daughters. They are depicted in a chariot pulled by galloping horses.

The Cenotaph, Whitehall
The word means 'Empty tomb'. The stark Portland stone column commemorates those who died in the two World Wars.

Charles I, Trafalgar Square
This is the oldest equestrian statue in London, dating from the 1600s.

Cleopatra's Needle, Victoria Embankment
This 60ft (18m) high granite obelisk from Heliopolis dates from 1475 BC. Erected in 1878, over a box and artefacts from that period.

Diana Memorial Playground, Kensington Gardens ♿
Six different play areas, accessible to all children.

Eros, Piccadilly Circus
Representing the Angel of Christian Charity, this aluminium statue is a memorial to Lord Shaftesbury.

London Peace Pagoda, Battersea Park
The only pagoda in London, and the only monument in Britain dedicated to world peace. Erected in 1985 by Japanese Buddhists.

London Stone, Cannon Street
Set into the wall of the Bank of China this piece of limestone is possibly a Roman milestone.

Marble Arch, north east corner of Hyde Park
This white marble arch stands on the site of the notorious Tyburn Gallows, which for over 400 years saw public hangings. The arch was designed as an entrance for Buckingham Palace, but it was too narrow for the state coach to pass through so was moved to its present site.

The Monument, Monument Street
This 202ft (61.5m) high portland stone pillar was designed by Sir Christopher Wren to commemorate the Great Fire of London. You can enjoy superb views by climbing up to the balcony via the 311 steps of the internal spiral staircase.

Nelson's Column, Trafalgar Square
The 145ft (44m) granite column was raised in 1843. It is surmounted by a statue of Admiral Nelson, who died at the battle of Trafalgar after defeating Napoleon.

Peter Pan, Kensington Gardens
This beautiful figure of the fictional character from J.M.Barrie's famous book was erected overnight in Kensington Gardens as a surprise for the children. The carved animals around the base have been partly worn away by children stroking them.

Queen Victoria Memorial, in front of Buckingham Palace
A white marble sculpture of Queen Victoria, surrounded by various allegorical figures. At the top is a gilded figure of Victory.

Sir Winston Churchill, Parliament Square
A powerful, modern bronze statue of one of Britain's great statesmen.

Wellington Arch, Hyde Park Corner
Archway erected in 1828 with sculpture added in 1912. Viewing platform and exhibitions inside. Open March to October.

Others to see
Achilles, Park Lane. **Sir Charles Chaplin**, Leicester Square. **Charles II**, Chelsea Hospital. **Oliver Cromwell**, Old Palace Yard. **Elizabeth I**, Fleet Street. **Mahatma Gandhi**, Tavistock Square. **Henry VIII**, St. Bartholomew's Hospital. **Sir Thomas More**, Carey Street. **Florence Nightingale**, Waterloo Place. **Sir Walter Raleigh**, Whitehall. **Richard the Lionheart**, Old Palace Yard. **Captain Scott**, Waterloo Place. **William Shakespeare**, Leicester Square. **Duke of York**, Waterloo Place.

◆ Bridges

Particularly noteworthy bridges across the Thames include:

Albert Bridge
Unusual rigid chain suspension, built 1873.

Chelsea Bridge
The original bridge was built in 1858 and was replaced by a suspension bridge in 1934.

London Bridge
The original bridge was made of wood and built by the Romans. In the 12th century, it was replaced by a stone one, incorporating shops and houses which was famous for displaying the heads of traitors. The present bridge dates from 1973, the previous one having been sold to Lake Havasu City, Arizona.

Millennium Bridge
London's newest bridge, with its 355 yard (325m) span, is a footbridge spanning the Thames from Bankside to St. Peter's Hill. It is a 'minimalist' stainless steel structure with a wooden walkway.

Tower Bridge
The architecture of this well known Victorian-Gothic bridge was designed to complement that of the nearby Tower of London. Completed in 1894, it opens in the middle to allow tall ships through. This was made possible by hiding a steel frame inside the granite and Portland stone. **The London Bridge Experience** provides a guided tour along the elevated pathways linking the two towers giving superb views of the city. The museum exhibition brings to life the human endeavour and engineering achievement which created this famous landmark. Open daily from 9.30am to 6pm. Adults £4.50, with concessions.
www.towerbridge.org.uk

Waterloo Bridge
Opened on the anniversary of the Battle of Waterloo, it was originally called Strand Bridge. It was replaced in 1942 by the present concrete structure designed by Sir Giles Gilbert Scott.

Westminster Bridge
This graceful bridge is cast iron and was built in 1854.

Other central London bridges spanning the Thames include **Battersea** (1890), **Blackfriars** (1860), **Lambeth** (1929) and **Southwark** (1921).

◆ Plaques

Since 1867, blue plaques have been used to mark buildings in London where famous people have lived and worked. The oldest surviving ones date from 1875. To have a blue plaque, the person must have been dead for over 20 years and have made 'some important contribution to human welfare or happiness'. There are now over 700 official ones; many 'unofficial' plaques also exist. English Heritage ☎ 020 7973 3000

Libraries & other institutes

British Library &
The national library of the UK welcomes visitors and has exhibition galleries, an events programme, a bookshop and tours of the building. Open daily from 9.30am (11am Sun). Reading rooms not open to the public without a reader's pass. Free entry to library and exhibitions. Tours, adults £6 - £7, with concessions. Phone for times.
96 Euston Road, NW1   ☎ 020 7412 7332 (visitor services)
www.bl.uk

Commonwealth Institute
Centre for Commonwealth education and culture.
Kensington High Street, W8   ☎ 020 7603 4535
www.commonwealth.org.uk

Family Records Centre
Indexes of births, marriages and deaths in England and Wales since 1837, and census returns since 1841. Invaluable for genealogical research.
1 Myddelton Street, EC1   ☎ 020 8392 5300
www.familyrecords.gov.uk/frc

Goethe-institut
Events reflecting German culture. Plays, exhibitions, films and more.
50 Princes Gate, Exhibition Road, SW7   ☎ 020 7596 4000
www.geothe.de/gr/lon/enindex.htm

Institut Français
A centre for French culture. Cinema, library, talks and wine tastings.
17 Queensbury Place, SW7   ☎ 020 7073 1350
www.institut-francais.org.uk

Parks & gardens

Since the second World War, there has been a concerted effort to increase the number of parks and green spaces in the city. There are some beautiful, tranquil retreats here, and the majority have free entry. For a leaflet ☎ 020 8472 3584.

◆ The Royal Parks

These were originally the grounds of Royal Homes or Palaces and are still Crown property. They are open to the public and free to enter.

Green Park
This park was once the meeting ground for duellists. The 53 acres of grass, flower beds and trees are perfect for a picnic.

Hyde Park
A Royal Park since 1536 and the most famous park in London. It contains a lake, the Serpentine, where you can hire a small craft or swim. You can wander and admire the various statues, or visit **Kensington Gardens**, the quiet end of Hyde Park, where you will find the Italian Fountain Gardens and memorials to the late Princess of Wales.

Regent's Park
Commissioned by Prince Albert, Regent's Park has a host of attractions including London Zoo, a heronry and waterfowl collection and an open air theatre. At the southern end are the beautifully laid out **Queen Mary's Gardens**.

St. James's Park
Alongside The Mall, this is the oldest Royal Park. It boasts a beautiful lake with an island which is home to a colony of pelicans. There are excellent views of Whitehall and Buckingham Palace. On a summer's day you can hire a deckchair and listen to music at the bandstand.

◆ Other gardens

Camley Street Natural Park, Camley Street
An interesting nature reserve, managed by the London Wildlife Trust.

Chelsea Physic Garden, Royal Hospital Road
Originally founded in 1673 to research the medicinal uses of plants; it also contains the oldest olive tree in Britain.
Adults £5, with concessions.

Finsbury Circus Garden, Finsbury Circus
A public garden with the only pagoda tree in London, as well as plane trees dating from the mid 1800s.

St. Mary Aldermanbury's Garden, Aldermanbury
A Victorian style knot garden incorporating the remains of Wren's church, medieval stonework and a bust of William Shakespeare.

Zoos & aquariums

London Aquarium ⏰ 💳 ♿
Everything aquatic, from a freshwater stream to the Atlantic Ocean.
Sharks, divers feeding conger eels and you can stroke the rayfish.
Open 10am to 6pm. Adult £8.75, with concessions.
County Hall, Westminster Bridge Road, SE1
www.londonaquarium.co.uk ☎ 020 7967 8000

London Zoo ⏰ 💳 ♿
With over 650 species, make sure you plan your visit so as not to miss a
favourite daily event. London Zoo also has a conservation and breeding
programme, helping to save some of the most endangered species on
the planet and in the Millennium Conservation Centre, the 'Web of Life'
explains the concept of biodiversity.
Open 10am to 4pm. Adult £12, with concessions.
Regent's Park, NW1 ☎ 020 7722 3333
www.londonzoo.co.uk

Spectator sports

◆ Cricket

Lord's Cricket Ground
Catch a test match, a one-day international or just a county game.
St. John's Wood, NW8   Credit card booking line ☎ 020 7432 1000
www.lords.org   For a tour ☎ 020 7616 8595/6
The Oval Cricket Ground
The home of Surrey County Cricket Club. The first test match in England
was played here in 1880. Watch international cricket or a home game.
Kennington, SE11   Credit card booking line ☎ 020 7582 7764

◆ Tennis

Wimbledon
Outside the area of this guide, Wimbledon is probably the best known
annual lawn tennis championship in the world. www.wimbledon.org
Honda Tennis Challenge
Top names playing in this December event.
Royal Albert Hall, SW7 ☎ 020 7589 8212

◆ Athletics

London Marathon
In spring, over 30,000 serious and 'fun' runners take to the streets of
London for this spectacular race.

Leisure activities

For **horse riding** in Hyde Park try **Hyde Park & Kensington Stables**, ☎ 020 7723 2813, or **Ross Nye Stables**, ☎ 020 7262 3791

Golf driving ranges are available at **Central London Golf School**, Clifton St., EC2 ☎ 020 7729 2300 and **Regent's Park Golf School**, Outer Circle, NW1 ☎ 020 7724 0643

For **ice skating**
Queens Ice Bowl, Bayswater, W2 ☎ 020 7229 0172
Somerset House Ice Rink is a courtyard, which between the end of November and January, is transformed into a huge ice rink. In the evening it is floodlit. Lessons available. ☎ 020 7413 3399
Broadgate Ice Arena is an outdoor rink near Liverpool Street station. Open between October and April. ☎ 020 7505 4068

Sightseeing tours

◆ Guided walking tours

The Original London Walks
Guided walks with many different themes from a St. Patrick's Day pub walk to The Beatles Magical Mystery Tour. Walks last about two hours. First walk around 10am, last at 7.30pm. 7 days a week. £5. Children under 15 free. Concessions £4.
www.walks.com   ☎ 020 7624 3978

Stepping Out
Specialising in smaller groups, guided walks include London City Ghost Walk, 2000 years of London history and Hidden London. A qualified London Guide is guaranteed.
£5. Concessions £4.   ☎ 020 8881 2933

Cultural Heritage Resources
These guided walks focus on the archaeology and history of London, with a bias towards the academic, whilst still being entertaining.
£5. Concessions £4.50
249 Evering Road, E5   ☎ 020 8806 3742
www.chr.org.uk

Personalised Walking Tours
Hire a 'Blue Badge' Guide; reputedly the best.
£81 half day, £121 full day.
www.touristguides.org.uk

◆ Self-guided walking tours

Silver Jubilee Walkway Self-guided 12 milee (19km) walk from Leicester Square to Westminster, with information plaques sited along the route. Map £1.50 from Visitor Information at Victoria Station.
London Wall Walk A walk along part of the Roman City Wall, with information panels.
Princess Diana Memorial Walk A seven mile (11km) walk through several of the Royal Parks. Plaques mark the route.

◆ Bus & coach tours

Original London Sightseeing Tour ⏱
Hop on, hop off service operating from Victoria Coach Station. Children's activities and a children's only channel of commentary. Daily. Adult £14, Child £7.50.
Jews Road, Wandsworth, SW18   ☎ 020 8877 1722
www.theoriginaltour.com

Harrods Luxury Sightseeing
Luxury open topped buses introduce you to the sights. Book at Harrods.
Knightsbridge, SW1   ☎ 020 7225 6596

The Big Bus Company
The 24 hour hop on, hop off ticket includes a river cruise, discounted entry to some attractions and four walking tours. Three departure points; Victoria, Marble Arch and Green Park. Daily Adult £15, Child £6.
48 Buckingham Palace Road, SW1   ☎ 020 7233 9533
www.bigbus.co.uk

Evan Evans
Operating since 1933. Pick up from over 60 hotels. Phone for prices.
258 Vauxhall Bridge Road, SW1   ☎ 020 7950 1777
www.evanevans.co.uk

◆ Car & taxi tours

London Taxi Tour
Ride in a London 'Black Cab'. Start from your hotel when you're ready.
4 Broadwall, SE1   ☎ 07957 2721791
www.blackcabtours.com

Concierge Desk
A tour of London designed for you, with all entrance fees and tickets organised. Book online.
PO Box 291, Horley, RH6 0FS
www.conciergedesk.co.uk

◆ Bicycle

London Bicycle Tour Company
A cheap way to see London without getting stuck in traffic.
1a Gabriel's Wharf, 56 Upper Ground, SE1 ☎ 020 7928 6838
www.londonbicycle.com

◆ River & canal trips

London Frog Tours
Amphibious vehicles drive along the road then into the river for part of
the 70 minute tour! Adult £15, Child £10, Concessions £13.00
County Hall, Westminster Bridge Road, SE1
www.frogtours.com ☎ 020 7928 3132

City Cruises
Daily sailings from Westminster, Waterloo, Greenwich or Tower piers.
Evening trips in summer. Adults from £6.30 return.
www.citycruises.com ☎ 020 7740 0400

The London Waterbus Company
Canal boat trips on Regent's Canal from Camden Lock or Little Venice.
Summer 10am and hourly to 5pm. Winter (Sundays only) 10am and
hourly to 3pm. Return, adult £5.50, child £3.50. With inclusive London
Zoo ticket £9.20 adult and £7.10 child.
Camden Lock, NW1 and Little Venice, W2. ☎ 020 7482 2660

London from the air

Adventure Balloons
An original way of seeing London, with champagne thrown in! Take off
sites all within a few miles of the Thames or the Tower of London.
www.adventureballoons.co.uk ☎ 01252 844222

Into the Blue
30 minute sightseeing flight by helicopter along the Thames. Flights go
from Biggin Hill airport, Kent 17 miles (27km) south of the City.
www.intotheblue.co.uk\helicopter-tour ☎ 01959 578101

London Eye ◔ ♿
On a clear day, you can see for 25 miles (40km) across London's famous
landmarks from the world's largest observation wheel. Open daily from
9.30am. Adult £11, plus concessions.
Belvedere Road ☎ 0870 5000 600 (credit card booking)
www.londoneye.com ☎ 0870 990 8885 (disabled booking)
☎ 0870 443 9858 (fast track tickets)
☎ 0870 220 2223 (private capsule sales)

Key to map pages

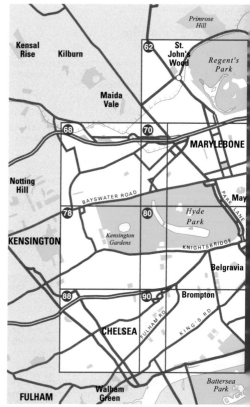

Scale
The maps on
pages 60 to 95
are at a scale
of 1:12,000
(approx 5¼ inches to 1 mile)

| 0 | 0.25 | 0.50 | 0.75 kilometre |

| 0 | ¼ | ½ mile |

Key to map symbols

Public transport
Transports publics   Öffentliche Verkehrsmittel

Main railway station
Gare ferroviaire principale   Hauptbahnhof

Other railway station
Autre gare ferroviaire   Anderer Bahnhof

VAUXHALL
⇌ **DLR**

London Underground station
Station de Métro Londonienne   Londoner U-Bahnhof

EDGWARE RD

London Underground lines - colour code
Lignes de Métro de couleur   Farbkodierung der U-Bahnlinien

Bakerloo ■	East London ■	Metropolitan ■
Central ■	Hammersmith ■ & City	Northern ■
Circle ■		Piccadilly ■
District ■	Jubilee ■	Victoria ■

Bus/Coach station
Gare d'autobus et autocars   Bus-/Reisebus Haltestelle

VICTORIA

Bus service terminal point
Terminal de la ligne d'autobus   Endstation der Buslinie

(12
31)

Regular daily service (bus routes & numbers)
Ligne quotidienne régulière   Regelmäßiger täglicher Dienst

2.36.185
88

One way bus route
Direction d'autobus   Einbahnstraße für Busverkehr ←

Places of interest
Visites interessantes   Sehenswürdigkeiten

Building open to the public
Bâtiment ouvert au Public
Gebäude-für die Öffentlichkeit zugänglich

Imperial War Museum

Other important building
Autre bâtiment important
Andere Sehenswerte Gebäude

Bank of England

Entertainment
Salles de spectacle   Unterhaltungsorte

Concert hall/Opera house
Salle de concert/Opéra   Konzertsaal/Oper   ROYAL OPERA HOUSE

Theatre   Théâtre   Theater   PALLADIUM

Cinema   Cinéma   Kino   ODEON

Shopping
Shopping   Einkaufsviertel

Principal shopping street
Principale rue commerçante   Haupteinkaufsstraße   NEW BOND ST

Shopping street
Rue commerçante   Geschäftstraße   Carnaby St

Major shop
Magasin important   Wichtiges Kaufhaus   Selfridges

Street market
Marché de rue   Straßenmarkt   ●

General information
Informations diverses   Allgemeine Informationen

Hospital   Hôpital   Krankenhaus   Guy's Hospital

Synagogue   Synagogue   Synagoge   ✡

Other place of worship
Autre lieu de culte   Andere Andachts/Kultstätte   +

Public toilet   Toilettes publiques   Öffentliche Toilette   WC

Tourist Information Centre
Syndicat d'Initiative   Touristeninformation   i

Major hotel   Grand hôtel   Wichtiges Hotel   Ritz

Public house   Pub   Kneipe   ★ Lamb & Flag PH

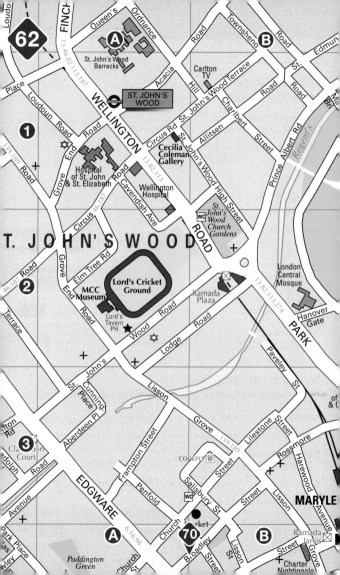

Terrace

Ormond Terrace

Prince Albert Road

WC

C

D

63

Canal

274

Outer Circle

Main Gate

London Zoo

Gloucester Gate

1

Regent's Park

WC

Broad Walk

Cumber Gate

WC

2

Inner Circle

OPEN AIR THEATRE

WC

Chester Road

64

Queen Mary's Gardens

Boating Lake

Bandstand

Inner Circle

Outer Circle

York Bridge

3

REGENT'S

Sq

Outer Circle

Kent Passage

Sussex

Circle

Royal College Obstetricians Gynaecologists

London Business School

Road

Place

Clarence Gate

Regent's College

Royal Academy of Music

London Clinic

Harley

Taunton Place

STEINER

Balcombe

Ivor

C Place

Gloucester

ROAD

Allsop Place

York Gate

Circle

18.27.30

Madame Tussaud's

Marylebone

St

Princess Grace Hospital

Devonshire Pl

Sherlock Holmes Museum

Dorset

Melcombe

St

Planetarium

ABC

MARYLEBONE

King Edward-VII Hosp

BONE

WC

2

Sq

Place

Luxborough

Nottingham

Beaumont

ROAD

PI

MARYLEBONE

BAKER STREET

ROAD

71

University of Westminster

D

Landmark

18.27

Sherlock Holmes

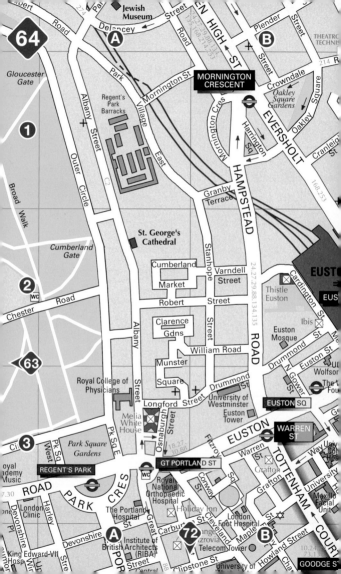

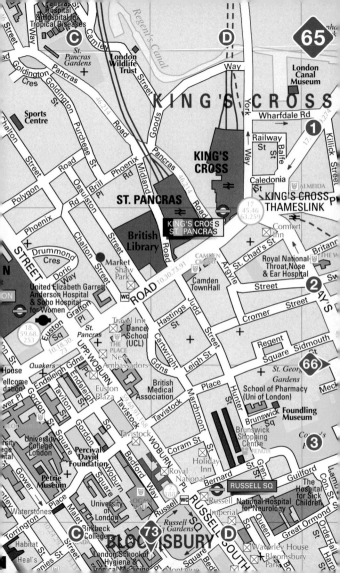

KING'S CROSS

Regent's Canal

Hospital & Hospital for Tropical Diseases

C

D

Camley Street

St. Pancras Gardens

London Wildlife Trust

London Canal Museum

Goldington Cres

Goldington St

Pancras Road

Sports Centre

Purchese St

Brill Pl

Phoenix Rd

Midland

Pancras Road

Goods Way

Way

York Way

Wharfdale Rd

1

Railway St

Balfe St

Killick

St

Chalton Street

Polygon

Ossulston Rd

KING'S CROSS

Caledonia St

ALMEIDA

KING'S CROSS THAMESLINK

Phoenix St

ST. PANCRAS

British Library

17, 45,46 63,259

STREET

Drummond Cres

Doric Way

Chalton Street

Market Shaw Park

WC

KING'S CROSS ST. PANCRAS

CAMDEN CENTRE

St Chad's St

Argyle

Royal National Throat, Nose & Ear Hospital

Britann

THE

Sw

United Elizabeth Garrett Anderson Hospital & Soho Hospital for Women

Grafton Pl

Camden Town Hall

Street

Street

Cromer Street

2

AY'S

18, 59,68, 253

Euston Sq

St. Pancras

Travel Inn

Dance School (UCL)

THE PLACE

New Ambassadors

Hastings St

Cartwright Gdns

Judd St

Leigh St

Regent Square

Sidmouth

66

10,18,30, 73

UPP. WOBURN

Quakers

Endsleigh Gdns

Endsleigh St

British Medical Association

Marchmont

Place

Hunter

St Georg Gardens

School of Pharmacy (Uni of London)

Meck

House

ellcome dation

Gordon St

Euston Plaza

Tavistock Square

Tavistock St

Coram St

Brunswick Square

Brunswick Shopping Centre

TRENOR

Foundling Museum

3

Coo's

University College London

Tavistock Square

Percival David Foundation

Gower

Bedford Way

WOBURN

Royal National

Holiday Inn

Bernard St

RUSSELL SQ.

National Hospital for Neurology

Great Ormond

Guilford

St

Con. Hosp.

Lamb

Con

The Hospital for Sick Children

Petrie Museum

rsity ge

ital

N

Waterstones

Torrington

Place

Malet St

University of London

SOA

Russell Square

RUSSELL SQ. SOUTH

Russell Gardens

Imperial

Waverley House

Bloomsbury

Queen

Great Ormond St

Habitat

Heal's

C

Birkbeck College

London School of Hygiene & Tropical Medicine

73

BLOOMSBURY

D

Southampton

Montague

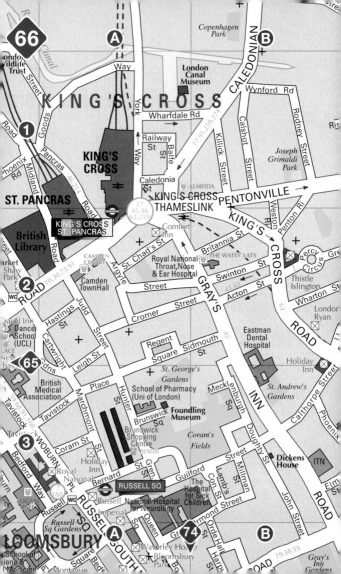

66

1

2

65

3

A

B

74

B

KING'S CROSS

Copenhagen Park

London Canal Museum

Goods Way

York Way

Wynford Rd

Rodney Street

Calshot Street

Killick Street

Joseph Grimaldi Park

Wharfdale Rd

17.91.259.274

Railway St

Balfe St

Caledonia St

ALMEIDA

KING'S CROSS THAMESLINK

KING'S CROSS

KING'S CROSS ST. PANCRAS

ST. PANCRAS

British Library

Phoenix Rd

Midland Road

Pancras Road

46.214

17
.45.46
63.259

PENTONVILLE

KING'S CROSS

Weston Street

Penton Ri

Percy Circus

Thistle Islington

Wharton St

Londor Ryan

Comfort Inn

Royal National Throat, Nose & Ear Hospital

THE WATER RATS

Britannia St

Swinton St

Acton St

45.63

Eastman Dental Hospital

Holiday Inn

GRAY'S

ROAD

ROAD

10.30.73.91

Camden Town Hall

St. Chad's St

Argyle Street

Cromer Street

Regent Square

Sidmouth St

45

Hastings St

Judd Street

Leigh St

Travel Inn

Dance School (UCL)

ACE Nev bas

British Medical Association

69.91.168

Tavistock

Cartwright Gdns

Marchmont Street

Place

Hunter St

St. George's Gardens

School of Pharmacy (Uni of London)

Mecklenburgh Sq

St. Andrew's Gardens

Calthorpe Street

Phoenix

INN

Market Shaw Park

WOBURN

Bedford Way

Coram St

Brunswick Shopping Centre

RENOIR

Brunswick Sq

Foundling Museum

Coram's Fields

Doughty St

Dickens House

ITN

Holiday Inn

Royal National

Bernard St

Guilford St

Lamb's Con. St

Millman Street

John Street

Elm

RUSSELL SQ

RUSSELL SQ

Imperial

Russell Sq Gardens

Russell National Hospital for Neurology

The Hospital for Sick Children

St. Green St

Queen Sq

Ormond Orde Hall St

LOOMSBURY

School of ena & Medicine

Montague

Square Bed

Waverley House Bloomsbury Park

ROAD

19.38.55

Gray's Inn Gardens

London Wildlife Trust

London Canal

7
488

WC

WC

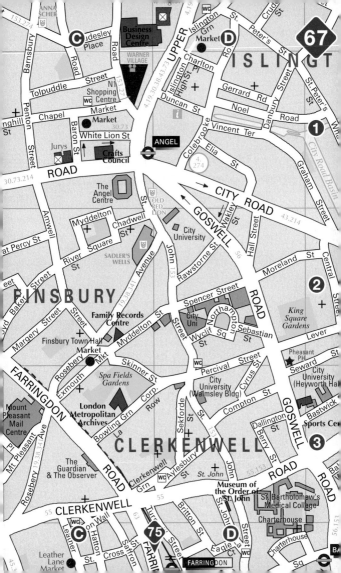

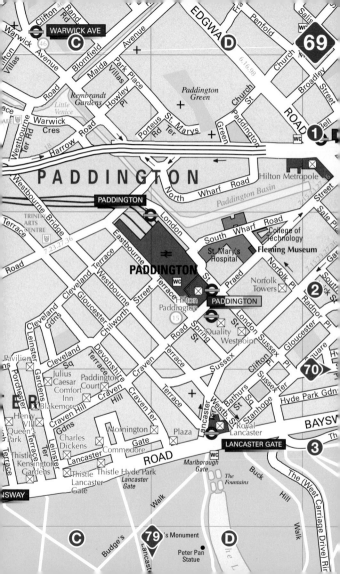

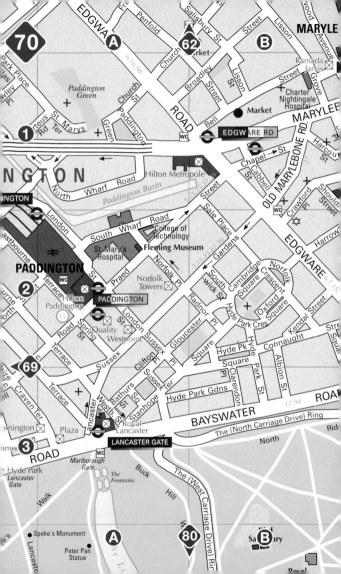

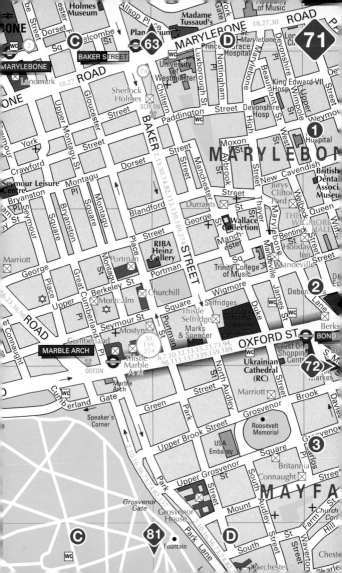

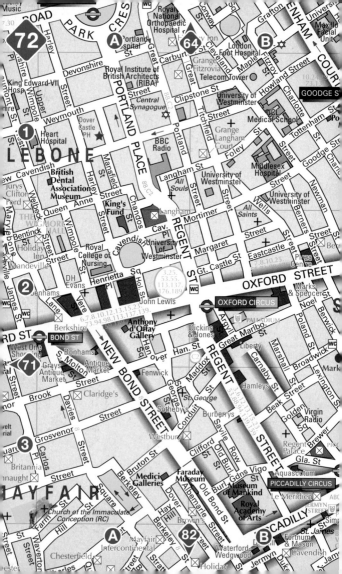

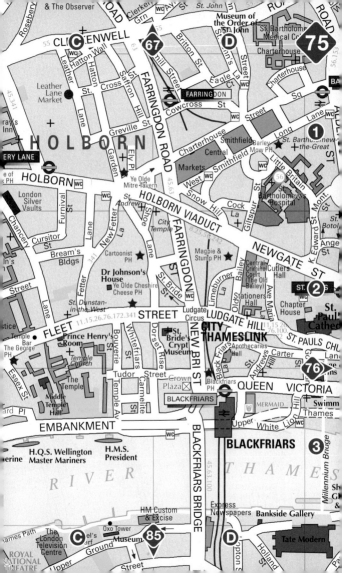

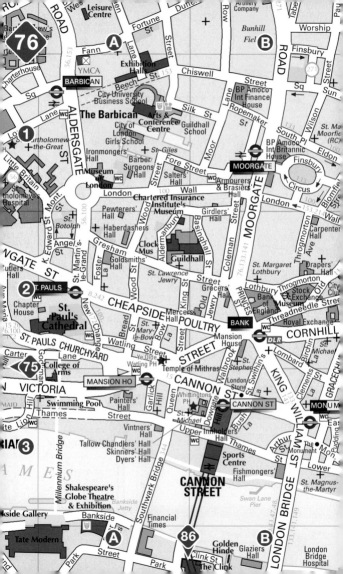

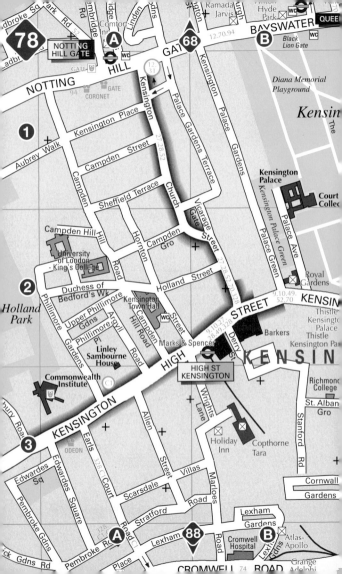

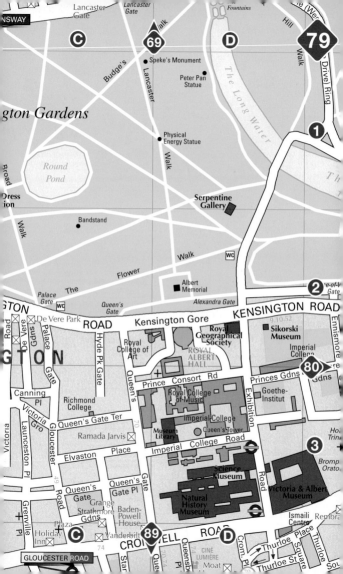

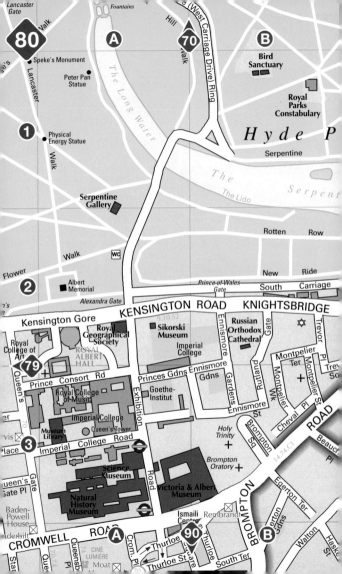

80 Lancaster Gate

Fountains

Lancaster Walk

Speke's Monument

Hill Walk

(West Carriage Drive) Ring

A

70

B

Bird Sanctuary

Peter Pan Statue

The Long Water

Royal Parks Constabulary

1

Physical Energy Statue

Walk

H y d e P

Serpentine

The

The Lido

Serpent

Serpentine Gallery

Rotten   Row

Walk

WC

New   Ride

Flower

2

Albert Memorial

Prince-of-Wales Gate

South   Carriage

's

Alexandra Gate

KENSINGTON ROAD   **KNIGHTSBRIDGE**

Kensington Gore

9,10,52

Royal Geographical Society

■ Sikorski Museum

Russian Orthodox Cathedral

Ennismore Gate

Trevor

Royal College of Art

ROYAL ALBERT HALL

Imperial College

Montpelier Ter

Montpelier Pl

Tre

So

79

+

Prince Consort Rd

Princes Gdns

Ennismore Gdns

Rutland Gate

Montpelier Wk

Cheval Pl

Montpelier St

+

Queen's

Royal College of Music

Goethe-Institut

Ennismore Gardens

ROAD

'vis

70

Imperial College

Museum Library

Queen's Tower

Ennismore St

Holy Trinity +

Brompton Sq

Beauc

Pl

Place

3

Imperial   College   Road

Brompton Oratory +

1474.C1

+

Science Museum

Road

Egerton Ter

Queen's Gate

Queen's Gate Pl

Natural History Museum

Victoria & Albert Museum

Egerton Gdns

Baden-Powell House

Ismaili Centre

Rembrandt

Walton

nderbilt

A

90

B

CROMWELL   **ROAD**

Queensl

Crom. Pl

Thurloe

Thurloe

South Ter

Hash

Sta

CINÉ LUMIÈRE

Thurloe St

Moat

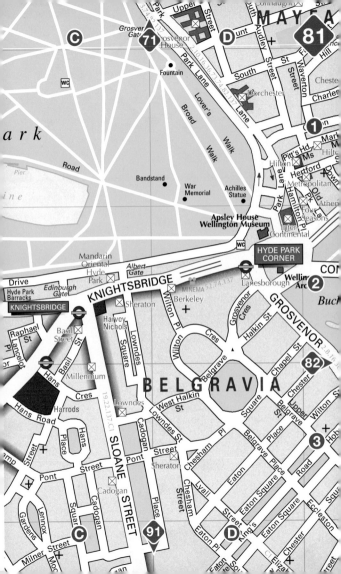

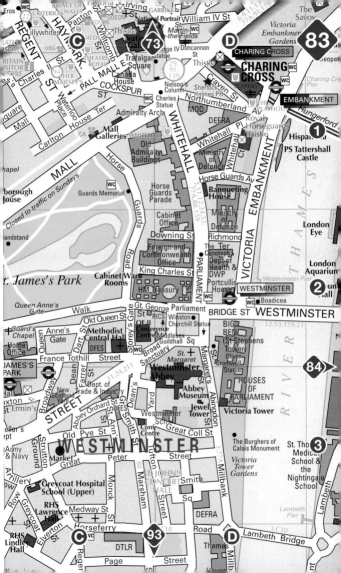

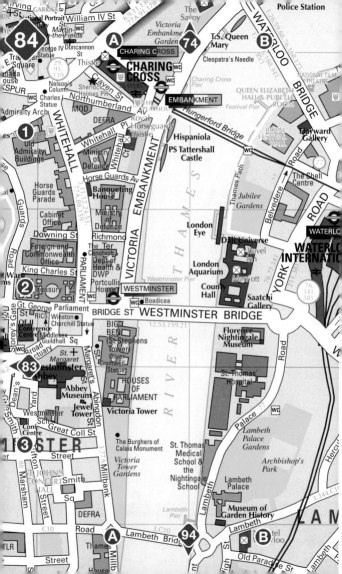

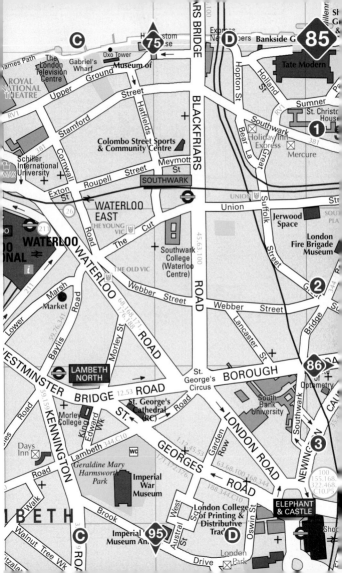

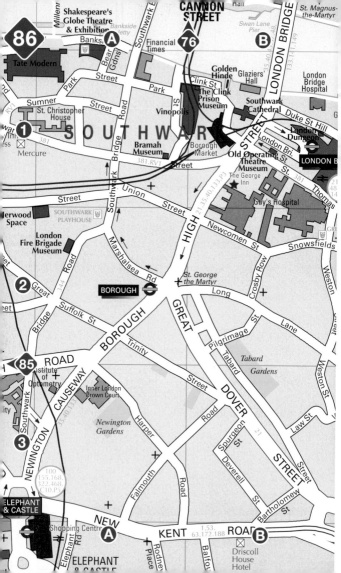

CANNON STREET

St. Magnus-the-Martyr

Swan Lane Pier

76

B

Shakespeare's Globe Theatre & Exhibition

Bankside Jetty

Banks...

A

Financial Times

Bear Gdns

LONDON BRIDGE

London Bridge Hospital

Tate Modern

Park

Street

Golden Hinde

Glaziers Hall

Clink St

The Clink Prison Museum

Southwark Cathedral

Duke St Hill

Sumner

Street

Park

Street

Vinopolis

Duke St Hill

London Dungeon

1

St. Christopher House

Southwark Bridge Road

Bramah Museum

Borough Market

London Bri.

LONDON B

Mercure

381

SOUTHWARK

381.RV1

Street

Old Operating Theatre Museum

St.

Thomas

The George Inn

48

Street

Union

Street

21.35.40.133.P3

HIGH

Guy's Hospital

GRE

erwood Space

SOUTHWARK PLAYHOUSE

Southwark

Marshalsea Rd

Newcomen St

Crosby Row

Snowsfields

Weston

London Fire Brigade Museum

Road

148

BOROUGH

St. George the Martyr

Long

Lane

St

2

Great

Suffolk St

BOROUGH

Trinity

GREAT

Pilgrimage

Tabard

Tabard Gardens

Weston St

Bridge

85

ROAD

CAUSEWAY

Institute of Optometry

Inner London Crown Court

35.40.133

NEWINGTON

Southwark

Street

DOVER

Road

Law St

3

Newington Gardens

Harper

Spurgeon St

Deverell

STREET

Street

Bartholomew

100 155.168. 322.468. C10.P5

Falmouth

Road

St

St

ELEPHANT & CASTLE

Shopping Centre

Elephant Rd

NEW

A

Rodney Place

KENT

Balfou

ROAD

1.53. 63.172.188

B

Driscoll House Hotel

ELEPHANT & CASTLE

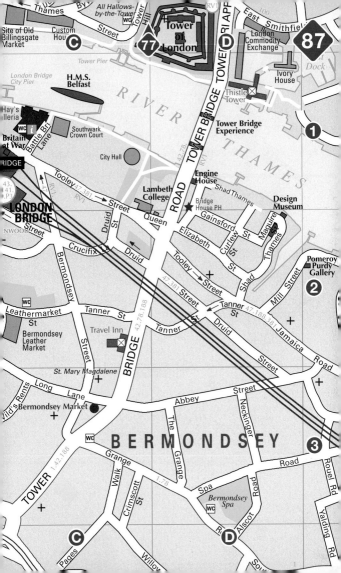

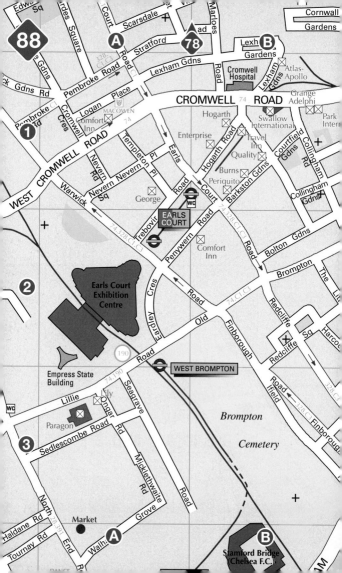

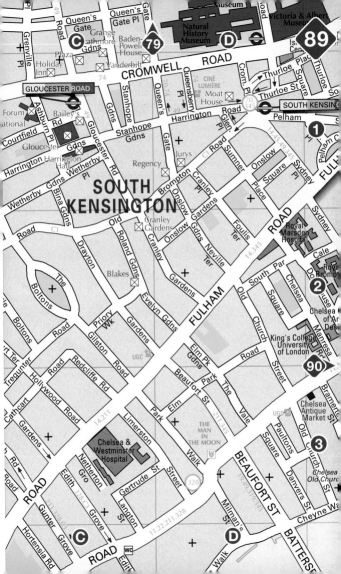

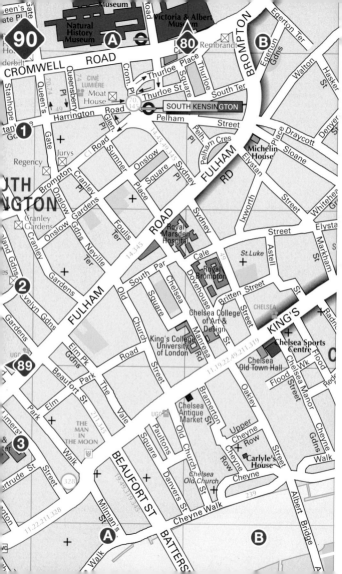

80

Museum

Natural
History
Museum

A

Victoria & Albert
Museum

Rembrandt

BROMPTON

Egerton Ter

Egerton
Gdns

Watton

Hasker

CROMWELL ROAD

Queensberry
Pl

CINÉ
LUMIÈRE

Moat
House

Thurloe
Place

Thurloe
Square

Thurloe St

South Ter

Crom Pl

SOUTH KENSINGTON

Pelham

Street

Pelham
Pl

Draycott

Denver

Stanhope

1

Queen's
Gate

Harrington   Road

Glen

Pelham Cres

Pelh
Pl

Sloane

Michelin
House

Jurys

Regency

Brompton

Cranley
Pl

Sumner

Onslow

Square

Sydney
Pl

FULHAM

RD

Elystan

Street

Ixworth

Whitehe

**UTH
NGTON**

Cranley
Gardens

Onslow Gardens

Cranley

Gardens

Onslow Gdns

Neville
Ter

Foulis
Ter

South Par

Sydney

ROAD

Royal
Marsden
Hospital

Cale

Royal
Brompton

St. Luke

Street

Astell

Markham
St

Elysta

2

Evelyn Gdns

FULHAM

Old

Chelsea
Square

Dovehouse

Street

Britten Street

CHELSEA

KING'S

Radn

Gdns

Church

Manresa
Rd

Chelsea College
of Art &
Design

Street

Sydney Street

Flood

Street

Chelsea Manor

C

89

Elm Pk
Gdns

Beaufort St

The
Vale

King's College
University
of London

Road

Chelsea
Old Town Hall

Chelsea Sports
Centre

Chelsea Wk

Elm

Park

THE
MAN IN
THE MOON

UGC

Chelsea
Antique
Market

Old Church

Bramerton
St

Upper
Cheyne
Row

Oakley

Flood Street

Cheyne

Gdns

3

Walk

Street

Paultons
Square

Danvers St

Chelsea
Old Church

Cheyne

Row

Carlyle's
House

Cheyne

Walk

Gertrude

328

BEAUFORT ST

Cheyne Walk

Albert

Bridge

Milman's

A

BATTERSEA

B

Walk

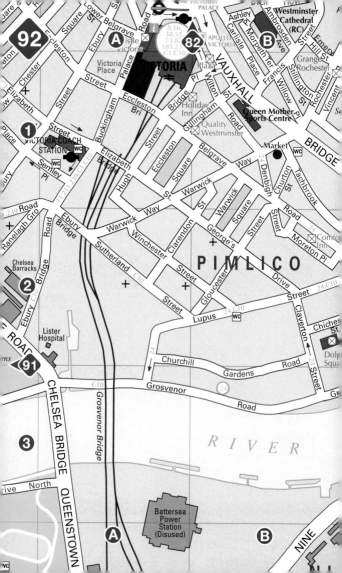

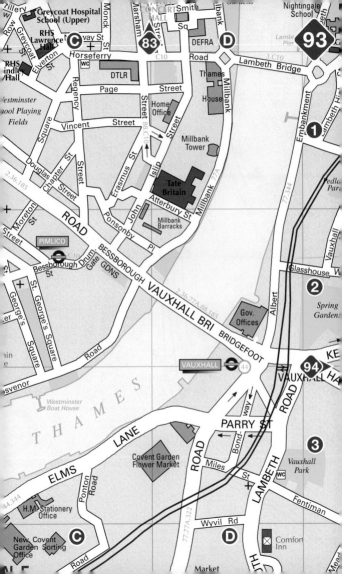

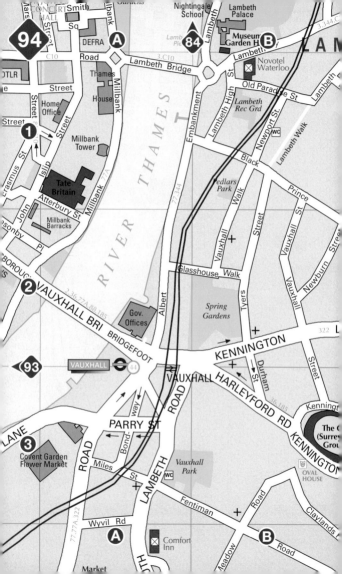

How to use this index

This index combines entries for street names, place names and other important features. Place names are shown in capital letters e.g. MAYFAIR. Street names are shown in black e.g. Oxford Street.

Other places are shown in blue and are distinguished by the following symbols:

●	Place of interest
⊞	Hospital
⇌	Railway station
⊖	London Underground station
▧▧	Docklands Light Railway station
⊠	Major hotel
♨	Theatre or concert hall
♨	Cinema
£	Important shop, shopping centre or market
▮	Tourist information centre

All entries are followed by the page number and map square where the name can be found.

Abbreviations used in this index

App	Approach	La	Lane
Ave	Avenue	Mkt	Market
Bdy	Broadway	Ms	Mews
Bldgs	Buildings	N	North
Bri	Bridge	Par	Parade
Ch	Church	Pk	Park
Chyd	Churchyard	Pl	Place
Circ	Circus	Rd	Road
Clo	Close	Ri	Rise
Cres	Crescent	S	South
Ct	Court	Sq	Square
Dr	Drive	St	Street
E.	East	St.	Saint
Embk	Embankment	Ter	Terrace
Flds	Fields	Twr	Tower
Gdn	Garden	Vill	Villas
Gdns	Gardens	W	West
Grd	Ground	Wd	Wood
Grn	Green	Wf	Wharf
Gro	Grove	Wk	Walk
Ho	House	Yd	Yard

97

109

111